Testimony of Hope

Dec. 2000

With warm Christmas
wishes for great blessings,

Sr. M. Beata, OSF

Testimony of Hope

The Spiritual Exercises
of John Paul II

By

Francis Xavier Nguyễn Văn Thuận

Translated by

Julia Mary Darrenkamp, FSP
Anne Eileen Heffernan, FSP

BOOKS & MEDIA

Boston

Library of Congress Cataloging-in-Publication Data

Francis Xavier Nguyễn Văn Thuận, 1928–
  [Testimoni di speranza. English]
  Testimony of hope : spiritual exercises of John Paul II / by Francis
Xavier Nguyen Van Thaun.
    p. cm.
  ISBN 0-8198-7407-8 (trade paper)
    1. Hope—Religious aspects—Catholic Church. 2. Spiritual
exercises. I. Title.

BX1795.H69 .N44 2000
269'.692—dc21

                                     00-063709

ISBN 0-8198-7407-8

Originally published in Italian by Cittá Nuova Editrice, Rome, under the title *Testimoni della Speranza.*

Cover design by Helen Rita Lane, FSP

Cover photo by Mary Emmanuel Alves, FSP

Printed and published in the U.S.A. by Pauline Books & Media, 50 St. Paul's Avenue, Boston, MA 02130.

Pauline Books & Media is the publishing house of the Daughters of St. Paul, an international congregation of women religious serving the Church with the communications media.

1 2 3 4 5 6 7 8 9   08 07 06 05 04 03 02 10 00

To His Holiness Pope John Paul II:
untiring witness of the hope
which comes from Jesus Christ,
he who has guided the Church
into the Third Christian Millennium,
on the occasion of his eightieth birthday.

Contents

9

Outside the Walls—All to All

HOPE AGAINST ALL HOPE

10

My God, My God, Why Have You Abandoned Me?

11

Can the Body Be Divided?

To Renew the Hope Within Us

To my mother Elizabeth
who educated me from the time I was in her womb.
She taught me stories from the Bible every night,
she told me the stories of our martyrs,
especially of our ancestors;
she taught me love for my country;
she presented St. Therese of the Child Jesus
as the model of Christian virtue.
She was the strong woman who buried her brothers
massacred by traitors, whom she sincerely pardoned,
always welcoming them as though nothing had happened.
When I was in prison, she was my great comfort.
She said to all, "Pray that my son will be faithful to the
Church and remain where God wants him."

God writes straight with crooked lines

I was summoned by John Paul II who said to me, "In the first year of the Third Millennium, a Vietnamese will preach the spiritual exercises to the Roman Curia."

Then looking at me intently, the Pope went on: "Do you have a theme in mind?"

"Holy Father, this comes to me from out of nowhere.... I'm surprised.... Perhaps I could speak about hope?"

"Present your own testimony!" John Paul II told me on that December 15, 1999.

Confused and deeply moved, I went home. I went into chapel and prayed, "Jesus, how am I going to do this? I'm not accustomed to speaking with a great deal of knowledge or theology. You know that I'm just an ex-prisoner."

"Speak from who you are. Do as the Pope told you. With humility, simplicity!"

So I thought of preparing a Vietnamese "cuisine." The cooking pot will be the same, so will the ingredients—the Gospel of hope—but I am changing the menu. I will use Asian seasonings and aromas, and it will be eaten with chopsticks. I will try to do my best, but a poor cook can do absolutely nothing without the fire: the Holy Spirit.

Asians do not argue their point with concepts, but tell a story or parable to make their meaning clear. That is how Confucius, Buddha, and Gandhi spoke; and that is how Jesus speaks:

A man was going down from Jerusalem to Jericho… which of these three, do you think, was a neighbor to the man…? Go and do likewise (Lk 10:30–37).

A former prisoner, who lived in a desperate situation or, rather, a more than desperate situation, has prepared this "menu of hope." He was believed dead, and the people offered many Masses for the dead for him. But, God knows how to write straight with crooked lines, and those Masses for the dead have borne the fruit of many more years of life.

Today, at the conclusion of the spiritual exercises, I feel profoundly moved. Exactly twenty-four years ago on March 18, 1976, on the vigil of the Feast of St. Joseph, I was taken by force from my residence in Cây Vông, and put in solitary confinement in the prison of Phú Khánh.

Twenty-four years ago I never would have imagined that today, on exactly the same date, I would conclude preaching the spiritual exercises in the Vatican.

Twenty-four years ago when I celebrated Mass with three drops of wine and a drop of water in the palm of my hand, I never would have dreamed that today the Holy Father would offer me a gilded chalice.

Twenty-four years ago I never would have thought that today (the Feast of St. Joseph 2000) in Cây Vông—the very place where I lived under house arrest—my successor would consecrate the most beautiful church dedicated to St. Joseph in Vietnam.

Twenty-four years ago I never would have hoped that today I would receive a substantial gift for the poor in this parish from a Cardinal.

God is great and great is his love!

To Jesus, to Mary, to Joseph,
to the Holy Father,
to all of you, dear brothers and sisters,
to the many people all over the world
who prayed for us in these days as in a great Cenacle,
I give infinite thanks.

I adore the manifestation of the divine mercy.

Pope John Paul II told me to publish these meditations, and I think that the letter signed by the Holy Father is the best introduction to them.

Francis Xavier Nguyễn Văn Thuận

March 18, 2000

POPE JOHN PAUL II'S
WORDS OF ACKNOWLEDGMENT

To Monsignor Francis Xavier Nguyễn Văn Thuận
President of the Pontifical Council of Justice and Peace

At the end of the spiritual exercises, which I and my closest collaborators of the Roman Curia had the joy of participating in during this first week of Lent, directed by you, our dear brother in the episcopate, my most cordial thanks for the witness of ardent faith in the Lord that you have vigorously expressed through your meditations on a very compelling theme for the life of the Church: "Testimony of Hope."

During the course of the Jubilee, I wanted to give a particular place to the witness of people who "have suffered for their faith, paying with their blood for their fidelity to Christ and to the Church, or courageously facing interminable years of imprisonment and privations of every kind" (*Incarnationis Mysterium*, n. 13). It is just such a witness that you have shared with warmth and emotion, showing that in the whole life of man, the merciful love of God, which transcends every human logic, is without measure, especially in moments of greatest anguish. You have brought us into contact with all of those who, in different parts of the world, continue to pay dearly for their faith in Christ.

Basing yourself on Scripture and on the Fathers of the Church, as well as on your personal experience and, in particular, your years spent in prison for Christ and his Church, you have brought to light the power of the Word of God which is, for the disciple of Christ, "the strength of faith for her sons, the food of the soul, the pure and everlasting source of the spiritual life" (*Dei Verbum,* n. 21).

Through your fraternal and stimulating words, you have guided us along the way of hope which Christ opened to us when he renewed our humanity, made us new creatures, and called us to an ongoing personal and ecclesial renewal. May the Incarnate Word give to every person who, even today, suffers so that Christ may be known and loved, the strength and the courage to announce the truth of Christian love to all people and in every circumstance!

Dear brother in the episcopate, I entrust you and your ministry to the maternal intercession of the Virgin Mary, Mother of Hope, so that through it you may contribute in a specific manner, in the name of the Church, to the establishment of justice and peace among people. May you receive the abundant grace of the Son, the Word Incarnate!

With all my heart, I impart an affectionate apostolic blessing, which I willingly extend to all those dear to you.

JOHN PAUL II

From the Vatican
March 18, 2000

WITH THE STRENGTH OF THE GRACE OF GOD

1

THE BOOK OF THE GENEALOGY OF JESUS CHRIST
Before the Mystery of God

I, Francis, servant of Jesus Christ, the least of the successors of the Apostles, here before you, do not believe that I know many things except Jesus Christ crucified. Obedient to the mandate of the Holy Father and with his blessing, I greet you, dear brothers, in *osculo sancto* ("with a holy kiss"), and I invite you, in the name of God, to begin the spiritual exercises of the year 2000 with this introductory meditation.

The genealogy of Christ

The Evangelist Matthew opens his testimony on Jesus Christ, the Son of God, with these words, "An account of the genealogy of Jesus Christ, son of David, son of Abraham..." (Mt 1:1).

The choice of this text as the subject of our first meditation may seem surprising.

When we deal with this Gospel passage during the course of the liturgical year, it is with good reason that we may feel a kind of embarrassment. Some might think that the reading of such a text is a meaningless exercise, an almost annoying repetition. Others simply read it rapidly, making it incomprehensible to the faithful; others abbreviate it by omitting some passages.

For Asians, and in particular for me as a Vietnamese, the remembrance of ancestors has an immense value. According to our culture, the book of one's family genealogy is kept with piety and devotion on the household altar. I myself know the names of fifteen generations of my ancestors going back as far as 1698, when members of my family received holy Baptism. Through our genealogies, we come to realize that we are part of a history greater than we are, and we welcome with greater truth the sense of our own histories.

For this I thank Holy Mother Church: that at least twice a year, during Advent and on the feast of the Nativity of Mary, we hear in our assemblies dispersed throughout the Catholic world, the names of many significant persons who, according to the mysterious designs of God, had an important role in salvation history and in the reality of the people of Israel.

I am convinced that the words of "the book of the genealogy of Jesus Christ" contain the essential announcement of the first and of the new covenant, the nucleus of the mystery of salvation which finds us—Catholic, Orthodox, and Protestant—all united.

Within the context of this holy Jubilee of the Incarnation, when the Church sings with joy its hope in Christ our only Savior, this passage of Scripture opens to us the mystery of human history as the mystery of mercy. It reminds us of what the Virgin Mary proclaims in her prophetic song, the *Magnificat*, and which the Church makes her own every day at the Vesper praises: the merciful and faithful plan of God is accomplished according to his promise made "to Abraham and to his descendants forever" (Lk 1:55). Really, the mercy of God extends and will extend from generation to generation, "because eternal is his mercy" (cf. Ps 99:5, 135).

The mystery of our call

The "book of the genealogy of Jesus Christ" is divided into three parts. In the first part the patriarchs are named; in the second, the kings before the Babylonian exile; in the third, the kings who came after the exile.

What impresses us immediately in reading the text is the mystery of vocation, of the choice on God's part, free and full of love, unbelievable according to the limits of human reasoning, and perhaps at times even scandalous.

Therefore, we read in the "book of the genealogy of Jesus Christ" that Abraham, rather than choosing Ishmael, his first born and the son of Hagar, chooses Isaac, his second born and the son of the promise, the son of his wife, Sarah.

In his own time, Isaac wished to bless Esau, his firstborn son, but according to the mysterious plan of God, in the end he blessed Jacob.

Jacob did not pass on the family line, carried forward historically to the Messiah. He did not choose Rueben, his firstborn. He did not choose Joseph the beloved and the best of all his sons, he who had pardoned his brothers and saved them from famine in Egypt. The choice fell to Judah, the fourth son, who was as responsible as the others for selling Joseph to slave traders headed for Egypt.

The disturbing mystery of God's choice concerning the ancestors of the Messiah begins to call for our attention. It also sheds light on the mystery of our own vocation.

"You did not choose me but I chose you" (Jn 15:16). We have not been chosen because of our merits, but only because of God's mercy. "I have loved you with an everlasting love," says the Lord (cf. Jer 31:3). This is our security. "The Lord called me before I was born, while I was in my mother's womb he called me" (Is 49:1). This is our boast, this awareness of having been called and chosen through love.

These days of retreat are an appropriate time to sing our infinite thanks to the Lord, "for his love is everlasting." From our hearts we should sing with great humility and gratitude, "He raises the poor from the dust, and lifts the needy from the ash heap, to make them sit with princes, with the princes of his own people" (Ps 113:7–8).

The mystery of sin and grace

If we consider the names of the kings in the "book of the genealogy of Jesus," we realize that before the exile only two of the kings, Hezekiah and Josiah, were faithful to God. The others were idolaters, assassins, and people without morals….

Even among the many kings mentioned in the post-exilic period, we find only two who remained faithful to the Lord: Shealtiel and Zerubbabel. The others are obscure figures or sinners.

In David—the most famous of the kings from whom the Messiah received his human origins—both sin and sanctity are mixed. With bitter tears, David confessed his sins of adultery and murder in the Psalms, especially in Psalm 50, which became the penitential prayer often used in the Liturgy of the Church.

In the beginning of Matthew's Gospel, even the women named as the mothers who gave life from the womb of God's blessing, arouse in us a certain emotion. They are all women who find themselves in strange situations. Tamar is a sinner, Rahab a prostitute, Ruth a foreigner. The Gospel does not even dare to name the fourth woman; she is simply "the wife of Uriah." Of course, this refers to Bathsheba.

Yet, the river of history, full of sinners and criminals, becomes a source of pure water as we approach the fullness of time. With Mary the mother and Jesus the Messiah, all generations will be renewed again.

This list of sinners' names presented by Matthew in the genealogy of Jesus does not scandalize us. Rather, it exalts the mystery of God's mercy. Even Jesus chose Peter who denied him and Paul who persecuted him. Nevertheless, they are still the pillars of the Church. If a people were to write their official history, they would certainly speak of victories, of heroes, of their greatness.... It would be a unique case, admirable and stupendous indeed, to find a people who would not hide the sins of their ancestors in an official history.

The mystery of hope

The entire Old Testament strains toward hope:

God comes to restore his kingdom.
God comes to re-establish the Covenant.
God comes to establish a new people,
to establish a new Jerusalem,
to construct a new temple.
God comes to recreate the world.

With the Incarnation, this kingdom has already come, and the end times have already arrived. However, Jesus also says that the Kingdom is growing slowly, secretly, like a mustard seed. Between the fullness of time and the end of time, the Church is on a journey as a people of hope.

The French poet, Charles Péguy, says, "The faith that I like the most is hope."[1] Yes, because in hope, faith, which operates through charity, opens new ways in the human heart. It moves toward the realization of a new world, of a civilization of love, and brings into the world the divine life of the most Holy Trinity, God's way of being and operating as manifested in Christ and transmitted through the Gospel.

---

1. Charles Péguy, *The Portal of the Mystery of Hope.* Abbeville: 1954, 81 Edition, p. 15.

This, brothers, is our great call. Not because we deserve it, but "because his love is everlasting." Today, as in the times of the Old and New Testaments, God acts in the poor in spirit, in the humble, in sinners who turn back to him with all their heart.

Crossing together the threshold of hope

As the theme for these spiritual exercises of the Jubilee Year 2000, I have chosen the title "Testimony of Hope." Hope is perhaps the greatest challenge at the threshold of the new millennium. *Witness to Hope* was the title of a recent biography of John Paul II. How could I not stop to thank the Holy Father for having guided the Church with his shining witness in *crossing the threshold of hope*? Passing through the Holy Door together with the members of other Churches and Christian Communities, crossing the threshold of the future, he has brought to light that all of humanity continues its pilgrimage toward Jesus who is our only hope.

Today I present myself as a humble ex-prisoner who has spent more than thirteen years in prison, nine of which were in solitary confinement. *Tremens factus sum ego et timeo* ("I became terrified and I tremble") also in facing this assignment that the Holy Father has entrusted to me. But I have taken comfort from an American novel about a famous preacher who captivated his listeners. In front of this preacher's pulpit always sat a little old man who faithfully followed his preaching. The preacher was thrilled with his success. One day, an angel appeared to him, "I congratulate you on the success of your sermons.... You really are great! But do you remember that little old man who always came to listen to you?" "Yes, I remember seeing him," responded the preacher. The angel said, "Then know that he came not to listen to you, but to pray for you. It is thanks to his prayers that your preaching has done so much good."

So, for this reason allow me to say that with all my heart I count on your prayers.

It is with such sentiments that we entrust ourselves to the Virgin Mary, *Redemptoris Mater,* Mother of the Redeemer, who in this chapel is enthroned among the saints of the East and the West. We feel her near to us as she was near the Apostles at Pentecost, almost as the very heart of the Church, as Mother of pastors and of the faithful, as Mother of the Church.

Nos cum prole pia benedicat Virgo Maria.

May the Virgin Mary bless us with her holy offspring.

HOPE IN GOD

2

Simon, Who Do You Say That I Am?
Jesus the Savior, Our Only Hope

In Saigon on August 15, 1975, the feast of the Assumption, I was asked to go to the President's Palace, the *Palace of Independence*. I was arrested there. It was 2:00 P.M. At the same time, all the priests and religious were summoned to the Opera House in order to prevent them from stirring up a reaction on the part of the people. So began a new and special stage of my long adventure.

I left the house dressed in my cassock, with a rosary in my pocket. During my trip to the prison, I realized that I was losing everything. The only thing I could do was to entrust myself to the Providence of God. Yet, in the midst of so much anxiety, I felt a great joy thinking, "Today is the Feast of the Assumption of the Blessed Virgin Mary into heaven."

From the day of my arrest, everyone was forbidden to call me "bishop, father." I was simply Mr. Văn Thuận. I could no longer carry any sign of my office. Without warning, I was asked, also on God's part, to return to the essentials.

Amid the shock of that new situation, face to face with God, I heard Jesus asking me this question, "Simon, who do you say that I am?" (cf. Mt 16:15).

In the prison, my non-Catholic companions wanted to understand "the reason for my hope." They asked me in all friendship and good will, "Why have you left everything—family, power, and wealth—to follow Jesus? There must be a very good reason!" My jailers instead asked me, "Does God really exist? Does Jesus? Is it a superstition? Is it an invention of the ruling class?"

So it became necessary for me to offer some explanation in a way that could be understood by these people, not with scholastic terminology, but with the simple words of the Gospel.

The defects of Jesus

Then one day I found a way of explaining myself. I ask your understanding and indulgence if I repeat here, before the Curia, a confession of faith that might sound more like a heresy: "I left everything to follow Jesus, because I love the defects of Jesus."

The first defect: Jesus has a terrible memory.

On the cross, during his agony, Jesus heard the voice of the thief crucified on his right, "Jesus, remember me when you come into your kingdom" (Lk 23:42). If I had been Jesus, I would have told him, "I certainly will not forget you, but your crimes have to be expiated with at least twenty years of purgatory." Instead, Jesus tells him, "Today you will be with me in paradise" (Lk 23:43). He forgets *all* the man's sins.

He does exactly the same thing with the sinful woman who has anointed his feet with perfume. Jesus does not ask her anything about her scandalous past. He simply says "her many sins have been forgiven because she loved much" (cf. Lk 7:47).

The parable of the prodigal son tells us that on the journey back to his Father's house the son prepares in his heart what he will say. "Father, I have sinned against heaven and before you; I am no longer worthy to be called your son; treat me like one of your hired hands" (Lk 15:18). Yet, when the father sees him from a distance he has already forgotten everything. He runs to meet him, embraces him, and does not even give him time to speak. He tells the servants who stand there stupefied, "Quickly, bring out a robe—the best one—and put it on him; put a ring on his finger and sandals on his feet. And get the fatted calf and kill it, and let us eat and celebrate; for this son of mine was dead and is alive again" (cf. Lk 15:23–24).

Jesus does not have a memory like mine. He not only pardons, and pardons every person, he even forgets that he has pardoned.

The second defect: Jesus doesn't know math.

If Jesus would have had to take a mathematics exam, he might have failed. He indicates this in the parable of the lost sheep. A shepherd has one hundred sheep. One of them becomes lost and, without delay, he sets out in search of it, leaving the other ninety-nine in the wilderness. Finding it, he puts the poor creature on his shoulders and returns to the fold (cf. Lk 15:4–7).

For Jesus, one is equal to ninety-nine—and perhaps more! Who could ever accept this? But his mercy reaches from generation to generation....

When it is a matter of saving the lost sheep, Jesus does not become discouraged by any risk or by any effort. We can contemplate his actions, full of mercy, when he sits beside Jacob's well and speaks with the Samaritan woman, or when he wishes to dine at the house of Zaccheus! What simplicity that knows no calculations, what love for sinners!

The third defect: Jesus doesn't know logic.

A woman who has ten silver pieces loses one of them and she lights a lamp to search for it. When she finds it, she calls in her neighbors and says to them, "Rejoice with me, because I have found the silver piece that I had lost" (cf. Lk 15:8–10).

This is truly illogical—to disturb your friends over one silver piece and then to plan a feast to celebrate the find! Even more, by inviting her friends, she is bound to spend more than the one silver piece. Not even ten silver pieces would be enough to cover all the expenses....

Here we can truly say, with the words of the French philosopher, Blaise Pascal, "The heart has its reasons that reason doesn't know."[1]

Jesus reveals the strange logic of his heart at the end of this parable, "Just so, I tell you, there is more joy in the presence of the angels of God over one sinner who repents" (Lk 15:10).

The fourth defect: Jesus is a risk-taker.

The publicity manager of a company or someone running an election campaign prepares a precise program, which includes many promises.

Nothing of the kind for Jesus! His publicity campaign, judged with a human eye, is doomed to failure.

Jesus promises trials and persecutions for those who follow him.

To his disciples who have left everything for him, he does not guarantee food or lodging, but only a share in his own way of life.

To a scribe who wants to join him as a follower, Jesus responds, "Foxes have holes, and birds of the air have nests; but the Son of Man has nowhere to lay his head" (Mt 8:20).

The Gospel passage of the Beatitudes, the true "self-portrait" of Jesus the risk-taker for the love of the Father and of humanity, is a paradox from beginning to end, even for us who have become used to hearing it:

---

1. B. Pascal, *Pensées*, n. 477, in *Oeuvres Compètes* (ed. J. Chevalier). Paris: 1954.

Blessed are the poor in spirit....
Blessed are the afflicted....
Blessed those who are persecuted for righteousness'
    sake....
Blessed are you when people revile you and persecute
you and utter all kinds of evil against you on my account.
Rejoice and be glad, for your reward is great in heaven
(cf. Mt 5:3–12).

The disciples had faith in this risk-taker. For 2000 years, and until the end of the world, the multitudes following Jesus will never be exhausted. It is sufficient to look at the saints of every age. Many of them belong to this blessed association of risk-takers—with no address, with no telephone, with no fax machine!

The fifth defect: Jesus doesn't understand finances or economics.

Recall the parable of the workers in the vineyard:

For the kingdom of heaven is like a landowner who went out early in the morning to hire workers for his vineyard and, after agreeing with the workers on a *denarius* for the day, he sent them into his vineyard. And when he went out about nine o'clock he saw others standing idle in the marketplace, and he said to them, "You go out into the vineyard, too, and I will give you whatever is just." So they went off. When he went out again at about noon and three o'clock he did the same. Now at about five o'clock when he went out he found others standing there.... He said to them, "You go into the vineyard, too." When evening came the lord of the vineyard said to his foreman, "Call the workers and pay them their wages, beginning from the last up to the first" (Mt 20:1–16).

If Jesus were named the administrator of a community or the director of a business, the institution would surely fail and go bankrupt. How can anyone pay someone who began working at 5:00 P.M. the very same wage paid to the person who has been working since early morning? Is this merely an oversight? Is Jesus' accounting wrong? No! He does it on purpose, as he explains, "Can I not do what I want with what is mine? Or are you jealous because I am generous?" (Mt 20:15)

And we have believed in love

Perhaps we can ask ourselves why Jesus has these defects. *Because he is love* (cf. 1 Jn 4:16). Real love does not reason, does not measure, does not create barriers, does not calculate, does not remember offenses, and does not impose conditions.

Jesus always acts out of love. From the home of the Trinity he brought us a great love, infinite, divine, a love that reaches—as the Fathers of the Church say—even to the point of folly, throwing our human measurements into crisis.

When I meditate on this love, my heart is full of happiness and peace. I hope that, at the end of my life, the Lord will receive me as he did the smallest workers in his vineyard. I will sing of his mercy for all eternity, forever in wonder over the marvels he has reserved for his chosen ones. I will be happy to see Jesus with all his "defects" which are, thanks be to God, incorrigible.

The saints are experts in this type of boundless love. In my life, I have often prayed to Sr. Faustina Kowlaska to help me understand the mercy of God. When I visited Paray-le-Monial, I was struck by the words that Jesus revealed to St. Margaret Mary Alacoque, "If you believe, you will see the power of my heart." Let us contemplate together the mystery of this merciful love.

You have made all things wonderfully

God created man and woman in his image, "You have made them a little less than the angels" (cf. Ps 8:6; Heb 2:7), giving them immortality, truth, justice.... The Second Vatican Council teaches:

> The dignity of man rests above all on the fact that he is called to communion with God. The invitation to converse with God is addressed to man as soon as he comes into being. For if man exists it is because God has created him through love, and through love continues to hold him in existence. He cannot fully live according to truth unless he freely acknowledges that love and entrusts himself to his Creator (*Gaudium et Spes,* n. 19).

In his freedom, however, man can refuse the *greatness* conferred upon him according to God's plan. He can seek to fulfill himself according to his own plans and pursue a different future than that promised by God. He can seek to guarantee his own future, as did the pagan nations—according to the testimony of Scripture—through the search for riches, reliance on human strength, covenants with powerful foreigners, and the possession of sacred things (cf. Hos 2:10; Ezek 16:15 ff.). Thus, humanity falls in its *misery*. It no longer hopes in God, but follows *false hopes*.

And more wonderfully have restored them

The Lord, especially through the prophets, does not cease to call men and women to the true hope that is Jesus, the only Savior. In Jesus we have been given the light of truth, the remission of sins, the restoration of freedom from the forces of evil, a new ability to love, participation in the divine nature, victory over death through the resurrection of the body, and life eternal. Jesus comes to meet human misery. Saving us, he made his Gospel and his grace the renewing principal of the world and, above all, of humanity in all areas of existence: private and public, cultural and social, political and economic. *To restore all things in Christ.*

In ecstasy before Jesus who is *Deus meus et omnia* ("my God and my all"), I desire to be, together with him, a source of hope in the garden of the world, as Charles Péguy writes:

> You may wonder, you may ask yourself: but how is it
> That this fountain of Hope flows eternally,
> Eternally young, eternally pure.
> Eternally fresh, eternally flowing.
> Eternally living….
> My good people, says God, it is not tricky.…
> If she wanted to make pure springs out of pure water,
> If she wanted to make springs of pure water,
> Then she would never find enough of it in (the whole)
>   of my creation.
> Because there is not a whole lot of it.
> But it is precisely with the impure water that she makes
>   her springs of pure water.
> And that is the reason she never runs out.
> But that is also why she is Hope….
> …and that is the most beautiful secret in the garden of
>   the world![2]

Hail, Mother of mercy,
Mother of God and Mother of forgiveness,
Mother of hope and Mother of grace,
Mother full of holy joy,
O Mary!

---

2. Charles Péguy, *The Portal of the Mystery of Hope.* Abbeville: 1954, 81 Edition, pp. 186–189.

3

GIVE AN ACCOUNT OF YOUR MANAGEMENT

Balancing Accounts at the Beginning of the Twenty-First Century

According to an ancient Asian tradition, a history of the Kingdom was compiled year by year at the Imperial Court. Two high ministers of the emperor were appointed to carry out this task. One had to write down the positive things that happened in the kingdom; the other had to make a list of all the negative things that happened. Neither of the two was aware of what the other was writing.

Then, at the beginning of the New Year, before the entire imperial court, the two scribes read their account in a special public audience. Everyone waited to learn the truth of the kingdom's state of affairs from the contrast between the two accounts.

After having heard the report, the emperor would turn to the court and invite, "Whoever has something to say, say it."

One year, when the emperor invited all to express their opinions, no one dared to speak. Absolute silence reigned until suddenly there was a moan and the sound of someone crying. The emperor demanded, "Who is crying? Whoever it is, come before me now and speak." A mandarin came out from the crowd, made a triple bow before the emperor, and said with great respect: "Majesty, no one in this court dares to speak the truth. I'm afraid that our nation is in great danger and risks downfall!"

We are invited to be searchers of and witnesses to the truth in hope, before the Lord and the world, for the good of the Church. On the first Sunday of Lent of the Jubilee Year 2000, the Holy Father gave the world an extraordinary witness and example by asking pardon of God for the mistakes and shortcomings of the sons and daughters of the Church throughout history. Then, offering pardon in his turn, the Pope encouragd us to accept the invitation to conversion.

The Lord invites us to conversion

If I dare to return to the invitation to conversion, it is because the Lord himself asks this of us. As to the administrators of his goods, he can repeat to us the words of the Gospel, "Give me an accounting of your management" (Lk 16:2).

The Lord asks of us a conversion *from* a negative or mediocre state *toward* one of a more authentic living of the Gospel. This means to abandon false hopes and, as servants of the petrine ministry, to put all our hope in Christ.

The Holy Father wanted to stress such a conversion with the Jubilee of the Roman Curia. This conversion is well suited to the spirit of the Jubilee and to the sense of life as a pilgrimage toward God, toward the light that illuminates and conquers our sins.

Let us not be afraid of our weakness. Even Peter was weak. It is truly the awareness of our fragility that keeps us authentic disciples of Christ and brings about an ongoing renewal in the heart of the Church.

Word of truth

Consider for a moment the many vast enterprises of the world. At the beginning of this new century, those in charge of such enterprises revised, in the light of recent "megatrends," their projects, the orientations of their activity, and the plans for their work.

On the threshold of the new millennium, we leave behind us a century of great conquests, but also of frightening disasters. We, too, desire to balance our accounts and to outline our possibilities in the light of the Word of God.

We are pastors of the offices of the Holy See with many people and tasks entrusted to our care. We belong to the Apostolic College. In communion with the Holy Father and under his authority, we share in the daily concern for the whole Church (cf. 2 Cor 11:28). How can we fail to ask the Lord to help us to grow in the spirit of conversion?

Have we been faithful, for example, to the correct fulfillment and realization of the will of God as manifested in the central event of our time, that is, the Second Vatican Council?

Nothing is more efficacious to enlighten and purify us than placing ourselves in the truth before the Lord himself, with immense love—he, with his Word of truth; the Risen One; the first and the last; the Living One. It is he who in every age speaks to the Church through his Spirit.

What the Spirit tells the churches

In the Book of Revelation, the Risen Christ draws up a balance sheet on the life of the seven churches of Asia Minor and speaks to their pastors. In synthesis, let us consider what the Risen Christ says and perceive in his voice the passion of Christ, the Spouse of the Church, for the sanctity of it's pastors and faithful.

The church of Ephesus: a church that has lost its first love (cf. Rev 2:1–7). The Lord reproves this church for no longer having that living love, always fresh and generous, which springs from the Holy Spirit and makes the church young again (*Lumen Gentium*, n. 4). "So think of where you have fallen from; repent and do the works you did before," the Lord says. Then he strongly admonishes, "If you do not, I will come to you and move your lamp stand from its place."

The church of Pergamum: a church that tolerates idolatry (cf. Rev 2:12–17). The Lord understands that this church lives in particularly difficult surroundings ("where Satan has his throne"). He appreciates its essential faithfulness, but the Word of God is "a two-edged sword." It is impossible to tolerate those members of the community who fall into idolatry. "So repent! If you do not, I will come quickly to you and make war against them with the sword of my mouth."

The church in Thyatira: a church that has given in to compromise (cf. Rev 2:18–28). This church is very hard-working and active. Yet, he who has "eyes of flaming fire" examines the purity of the heart. Compromises in morality do not escape him. "You tolerate Jezebel, who claims to be a prophetess. She teaches and misleads my servants, so that they commit fornication…. I gave her time to repent, but she will not repent…." The Lord will give authority over the nations only to those who have integrity of life "until the end."

The church of Sardis: a church that sleeps (cf. Rev 3:1–6). "I know you are considered to be alive, but you are dead. Wake up! Strengthen what remains to you but is on the verge of dying." Of this church, Jesus asks that they not rely on the glories of the past, but rather "remember what it was that you heard and received…hold fast to it and repent! If you do not wake up I will come like a thief…."

The church of Laodicea: a tepid church (cf. Rev 3:14–22). Now we encounter perhaps the strongest of reproofs: "You are neither hot nor cold. Would that you were either hot or cold! And so, because you are lukewarm and neither hot nor cold, I will vomit you out of my mouth!" The Lord rejects mediocrity. The saints say that this is the most dangerous state in the spiritual life. Jesus wants to pull us out of our mediocrity, and he does this with the invitation to listen to him who knocks at the door of our life. "For you say, 'I am rich, and have become wealthy; I need nothing,' not realizing that you are wretched—miserable and poor, blind and naked.... So be zealous and repent."

Of the seven churches, the Risen Christ reprimands five for their lack of ardent love, for compromises, for idolatry, for sleeping, and for tepidity. Only two churches are not reproved: Smyrna and Philadelphia.

The church in Smyrna: a church persecuted and poor (cf. Rev 2:8–11). The Risen One encourages the church in its moment of trial and testing: "I know of your suffering and your poverty, but you are rich.... Do not fear what you are about to suffer. Behold, the Devil is going to throw some of you into prison in order to test you.... Be faithful unto death." In this way, one receives the crown of glory.

The church of Philadelphia: a church small but faithful (cf. Rev 3:7–13). Already the name of this Church, *philadelphia,* "brotherly love," is significant (cf. 1 Pet 1:22; 2:17). Such is the term used in the New Testament to speak of the love that the disciples of Jesus have for one another. For this Church the Lord has a special word of encouragement: "I have set before you an open door, which no one can close." It is a small church, but beloved of God: "I know that your power is not great, yet you have kept my word and have not denied my name.... I will protect you in the time of trial."

Let us look at some other elements that recur in each of these messages: "I know your works...."; "I know where you live...."; "I know your tribulations...." The Lord knows each of us. He penetrates our life with his gaze that is like a flame of fire, and he calls us to re-examine our relationship with the One who is "the first and the Last."

In each church, he who is just finds reason for giving praise, but to almost all of them he also says: "I have this against you...." These are words which do not leave the churches indifferent. Christ's love is too ardent to allow the Church to stagnate in her weakness. His appeal to conversion is insistent, heartbreaking, sustained by a love that is discreet but does not allow a truce.

Each message concludes with the words, "Let anyone who has an ear listen to what the Spirit is saying to the churches." Our journey of conversion finds its summit and completion in this listening to the Spirit. We, his Church, must abandon ourselves entirely to him. He will give us the grace to respond fully to his call, and the capacity to read the signs of the times. This is the aim of the Jubilee.

I think that the last message is the compendium of what the Lord desires to say to his Church: be a Church faithful to love, faithful to the word of the Gospel, faithful to the law of brotherly love! Then you will be a witness of the presence of the Lord, you will grow, and live, and conquer!

We come, Lord: with humility in the presence of God

There is a prayer attributed to St. Isidore of Seville[1] that we recite frequently at those special occasions when we are together: *Adsumus Domine* ("Here we are, Lord").

Every time I pray these words, I feel both challenged and urged to live in truth before God. It penetrates me with the particular light of the will of God.

I recite it and feel I am in the presence of God, of the God before whom we are when we pray, *"Adsumus."*

Like a litany, this prayer serves as purification and places me again in humility. *Peccati quidem immanitate detenti* ("we are before you with our load of sin").

---

1. Cf. *La Preghiera dell'Adsumus. Note Storico–Critiche*, in: D. Balboni, *Anecdota Liturgica*, I. Cittá del Vaticano: 1984, pp. 17–24.

We feel encouraged and, as on a seesaw, we rise again from the abyss of our misery to the heights of divine mercy. *Veni ad nos, et esto nobiscum* ("come in our midst and stay with us").

We entrust ourselves to the Lord's guidance in order to find the straight road of his will. *Doce nos quid agamus, quo gradiamur, quid efficere debeamus* ("teach us what to do, how to proceed, and what we have to carry out").

What might be the sins and defects we ask to be freed from by the power of the Holy Spirit?

Perhaps there is a lack of justice in our work if we are "disturbers" of justice.

If only our lack of objectivity in judgment and decisions, of an accurate study of the problems at hand, of attention to the truth, of the exercise of discernment, "if only ignorance would not drag us into error" *(non in sinistrum ignorantia trahat).*

Perhaps our human fragility weakens us so that we yield to favors received, or allow our need for the esteem of the powerful to gain the upper hand. Perhaps it conditions our judgments to seek the approval of others, even at the risk of consenting to a certain level of corruption. All of this is said with humility, to the point of feeling uneasy in being obliged to say, *non favor inflectat, non acceptio muneris vel personae corrumpat* ("popularity does not influence, nor does the acceptance of a gift or person corrupt").

We are invited to ask ourselves if there is always a passion for the truth in us, an honest search to use all possible means in order not to deviate from the right way.

Let us have only one desire: to be interpreters and faithful administrators of the will of God in our words and in our actions, *ut a te in nullo dissentiat sententia nostra* ("that our decisions may never in any way stray from you").

The more we are friends and servants of God—the more aware we are of having been chosen and honored to render God a competent service in the Church and for the world—so much more must we be impassioned to maintain unity of heart, *ut simus in te unum* ("that we may be one in you"). And thus, we will be heard because we are united in the name of the Lord, according to his promise, *in nomine tuo specialiter congregati* ("especially gathered in your name") (cf. Mt 18:20). Living in the presence of God, we turn to him, as his beloved children—like Jesus—with a simple prayer that God alone be the one who suggests to us what we must speak and what we must do.

With an immense faith of always having—if we ask with profound humility—the grace of God to sustain us in affective and effective communion with him, we pray, *Iunge nos tibi efficaciter solius tuae gratiae dono* ("bind us strongly to you by the gift of your grace alone").

Called to make an examination of conscience and to give an account at the end of this century and at the beginning of a new millennium, the prayer "Here we are, Lord," recalls us to the work of constant renewal, even under an ecclesial aspect in our concrete service to the Holy Father in his petrine ministry.

In his first letter, St. Peter gives us advice on this point, "Always be ready with a reply for anyone who demands an explanation for the hope you have within you, your defense to anyone who demands from you an accounting for the hope that is in you; but do it humbly and respectfully and have a clean conscience" (1 Pet 3:15–16). Converting ourselves to the full measure of our call at every moment, we will truly cross the threshold of the Holy Door that is the living Christ in and among us, with the desire to live as Jesus lived for the Father, moved always by the Spirit, to do always and in all things the will of the Father, *ut tibi in omnibus placere vale-amus* ("so that we can please you in everything").

Come, Lord Jesus!

I would like to conclude this meditation with a word and a prayer of hope.

When I was in Melbourne, Australia, to preach a course of spiritual exercises, I read these words of hope with great consolation: "There is no saint without a past, there is no sinner without a future...."

We are before the Lord who has reunited, in his name, all our past in his mercy and all our future in his immutable fidelity.

This prayer of hope is suggested by St. Ambrose, a pastor who prays to Jesus the Good Shepherd with these words:

Come therefore, Lord Jesus,
search for your servant,
search for the lamb you espoused.
Come, Shepherd, search, as Joseph looked for his sheep.
Your sheep went astray as long as you lingered,
as long as you enjoyed yourself in the mountains.
Leave your ninety-nine sheep and come to look for the
one who has gone astray.
Come without dogs, come without rough hired hands,
come without mercenaries who do not know
how to pass through the door.
Come without helpers, without intermediaries; for a long
time already I have been waiting for your coming.
I know that you are going to come, if it is true that I have
not forgotten your commandments.

Come, but without the staff;
come with love instead and
    with an attitude of mercy.[2]

The Church is not renewed once and for all; it is renewed every day.

May the Lord, the Good Shepherd, come thus to convert us and renew us!

---

2. *Dal Commento al Salmo,* 118, 22, 28: PL 15, 1599.

4

FOR GOD SO LOVED THE WORLD
The World of Today

For God so loved the world
  that he gave his only begotten Son,
So that everyone who believed in him
  would not die but would have eternal life.

For God did not send his Son
  into the world to judge the world,
But so the world would be saved
  through him (Jn 3:16–17).

In these two verses from the fourth Gospel resound, as Pascal says, all the greatness and the misery of man.

At the beginning of his pontificate the Holy Father affirmed in his encyclical letter *Redemptor Hominis* that "man… is the primary and fundamental way of the Church" (n. 14). In the encyclical *Dives in Misericordia,* he also wrote: "In Jesus Christ, every path to man, as it has been assigned once and for all to the Church in the changing context of the times, is simultaneously an approach to the Father and his love" (n. 1).

And in the Pastoral Constitution *Gaudium et Spes,* the Second Vatican Council described the condition of man in the modern world, a world that "God has so loved" and for which Jesus paid a very dear price:

Since all these things are so, the modern world shows itself at once powerful and weak, capable of the noblest deeds or the foulest; before it lies the path to freedom or to slavery, to progress or retreat, to brotherhood or hatred (n. 9).

Faced with this situation today, the Church must listen to the world's cry for help. At the same time, it must look to the light of truth received from God to discern hopes and threats, preoccupations and reasons for anguish—in a word, to discern the lights and shadows.

I think that no one has better synthesized the condition of the world than Paul VI in his *Testament:*

I close my eyes to this sorrowful land, dramatic and magnificent, calling down once more upon it the divine goodness.[1]

This magnificent land

The first four words of the Pastoral Constitution of the Second Vatican Council are: *"Gaudium et spes, luctus et angor"*—joy and hope, sadness and anguish.

Let us begin with the joys and hopes, with the lights.

The first half of the last century saw two world wars, which caused unheard of suffering, millions upon millions of victims, and enormous destruction never witnessed before. Beginning with the second half of the last century, the world lived many years in the nightmare of a Cold War between two ideological blocks and under the constant threat of nuclear war. In Europe, the fall of totalitarian regimes—which according to the *Black Book of Communism* were respon-

---

1. "Testament of Paul VI," June 30, 1965, n. 6. *L'Osservatore Romano,* Aug. 12, 1978, p. 2.

sible for 100 million victims[2]—opened new prospects for world peace.

We can note with joy the considerable progress made:

- child mortality has diminished by half since 1965;
- life expectancy is up by ten years since 1970;
- attendance at primary and secondary schools has more than doubled;
- adult literacy has gone from less than 50 percent to more than 70 percent;
- the medium income per capita has more than tripled in the last fifty years.

Crossing the threshold of the third millennium, humanity is encouraged by the growing awareness of universal human rights, the sense of the rights of a people to self-government, appreciation of cultural identity, respect for minorities, and the general positive perception of the value of democracy and free market.

Religions are always more determined to carry out roles of dialogue and reconciliation, which are fundamental elements of peace and unity.

The promotion of woman finds itself supported in both civil society and in the Church.

Responsibility toward the created world illumines an awareness of God's gift with a new light.

The great progress in the means of communication, in medicine, and in science are motives of hope for the well-being of humanity and of gratitude to the Creator.

In the spiritual dimension, a great reawakening, a new search for interiority and authenticity can be observed in

---

2. Stéphane Courtois, Nicolas Werth, Jean Louis Panné, Andrzej Paczkowski, Karel Bartosek, Jean Louis Margolin, *Le Livre Noir du Communisme: Crimes, Terreur, Repression*. Paris: 1997, p. 14.

significant contexts. The "fame" of prayer and of encountering the Absolute grows.

Globalization is, in some ways, contributing to the future of a more united world that is jointly responsible and educates toward recognizing a human family.

Like a fresh springtime in the Church, new ecclesial movements are flourishing with their witness of joy in faith, in hope, and in love.

This sad land

Seeing humanity enter the Third Millennium with such great possibilities for peace and progress raises our spirits and encourages us. In my daily work, however, I observe that many people suffer because they are marginalized, discriminated against, and their human dignity is not respected. There is many a "Lazarus" around the table of the rich, people who are afflicted with poverty and medical and social instability. There is many a "Lazarus" in the world eating whatever leftover food is found in the streets from the plates of those dining in restaurants. Unimaginable things!

According to the World Bank:

- 1.3 billion people live beneath the threshold of absolute poverty;
- 840 million people suffer hunger, 200 million of whom are children;
- 13 million people are condemned to death every year—that means almost 36,000 a day, 1,500 every hour, 25 every minute, and 1 every 3 seconds.

Approximately 1.5 billion of the world's population has a life expectancy of less than 60 years, more than 880 million have no access to health services, and 2.6 billion lack the most basic sanitary structures.

Between 1990 and 1997, the number of individuals affected by the AIDS virus rose from less than 15 million to more than 33 million.

> All this is happening against the background of the gigantic remorse caused by the fact that, side by side with wealthy and surfeited people and societies, living in plenty and ruled by consumerism and pleasure, the same human family contains individuals and groups that are suffering from hunger. There are babies dying of hunger under their mothers' eyes.[3]

Poverty generates many other social miseries such as prostitution, which involves 500 thousand women in Western Europe alone; drug trafficking among children; widespread violence and crimes. A lack of employment is the root cause of many suicides among desperate young people.

In these past few years, especially within the context of the Great Jubilee, John Paul II has asked that international debts be canceled, or at least that the vicious spiral of debt among underdeveloped countries be reduced. The most obvious example is Africa. Although sub-Saharan Africa paid its debts to the West twice between the years 1980 and 1996, today it finds itself three times more indebted than sixteen years ago.

Cultural insecurity is a distinctive face of poverty. In 1997, more than 8.5 million adults were illiterate and more than 260 million children were excluded from elementary and secondary education.

The illegal marketing of drugs, weapons, and the circulation of laundered money are frequently causes of war. Between 1989 and 1998 there were eighty-one armed conflicts—three between different countries, and seventy-eight civil wars. Millions of young men—beginning from the age

---

3. John Paul II, *Dives in Misericordia* (On the Mercy of God). Boston: Pauline Books & Media, 1980, n. 11.

of fourteen—were mobilized by force and sent as soldiers to fight in wars. Many have died, others are now handicapped, and still others have become accustomed to hate, violence, massacres….

The scene of the Mount of Olives comes to mind where, facing the city of Jerusalem, the Lord wept at the sight of his city. If Jesus were to pass through this "sorrowful and dramatic" world today, he would surely cry and exclaim, "*Misereor super turbum*" ("I feel compassion for these people").

In so many places Christ is still crucified and he cries out, "I thirst."

This dramatic land

In spite of the encouraging progress that has been witnessed during this period of globalization, the gap between the rich and the poor becomes greater every day.

It is incredible when one stops to consider that the total wealth of the three richest individuals in the world equals the gross national product of forty-eight of the poorest nations. While Bill Gates earns 120 million dollars every day, 1 billion and 300 million people are living on less than a dollar a day.

It is a disturbing fact that 88 percent of all internet users live in industrial countries, while 2 billion people still lack electricity; and that 20 percent of the world's wealthy population consumes 86 percent of all its goods.

Another dark area of our world is the whole sphere of the moral worth of the human person in his interiority and subjectivity. A dangerous moral relativism exists, a "cancerous development of subjectivity"[4] that promotes de-Christianization, practical atheism, and the reduction of faith entirely

---

4. C. M. Martini, *Qualche anno dopo*. Casale Monferrato: 1987, p. 37.

to the private sector. Yet, at the same time, various religious sects and fundamentalist groups proliferate. If in the past the Church suffered strong crises in the area of faith, in our time the crisis is in the area of morals. The truth of the human person is obscured, and so the family disintegrates, the order of creation is twisted, freedom is abused, and life is not respected.

Urbanization creates new pastoral problems. By the year 2015, one out of every five Frenchmen will live in the region of Paris. In many nations, whole regions are being depopulated due to the lack of available work. In many countries, the growth of the aging population will make their social security systems explode.

Within fifteen years, the working class in many European countries will diminish enormously, just as has the farming class. In 1984, workers in France numbered 8.2 million, today they number 6.2 million, and by 2015, the number is expected to fall to 4 million. The society of the future will be more than 75 percent employees and middle managers.

On-line services have made profound changes to our life—every good and every evil reach into the intimate heart of the family. Countries under dictatorships can no longer be entrenched behind walls, barriers, and prohibitions.

All these social changes have a tremendous impact on the People of God. Pope John XXIII's firm conviction comes to mind: if the Church does not go out to meet humanity, humanity will not come to meet the Church.

We announce with great joy: the Savior is born for us

Amid the shadows and gloom of today's world, the words of Isaiah read by Jesus in the synagogue of Nazareth resound strongly in our hearts and minds:

The Spirit of the Lord is upon me,
because he has anointed me
to bring the good news to the poor,
he has sent me to proclaim release to the captives
and recovery of sight to the blind,
to set at liberty the oppressed,
to proclaim the acceptable year of the Lord
(Lk 4:18–19).

The Great Jubilee brings us the hope of a strong renewal with the grace of a new Pentecost. Without a conversion of heart, a good part of humanity risks passing from the experience of exploitation to exclusion, and from exclusion to true and proper elimination—perhaps even physical.

Paul VI's vision of a "sorrowful land, dramatic and magnificent" does not leave me in peace. I dream of a great hope.

I dream of a Church that is the *Holy Door*, always open, embracing all, full of compassion; and that understands the pains and sufferings of humanity, protecting and consoling all people.

I dream of a Church that is *Word*, manifesting the book of the Gospel to the Four Corners of the world in a gesture of announcement, of submission to the Word of God as the promise of the eternal Covenant.

I dream of a Church that is *bread*, eucharist, that allows itself to be eaten by all people in order that the world may have abundant life.

I dream of a Church that is passionate for the *unity* that Jesus desired (cf. Jn 17), like John Paul II, who opened the Holy Door of the Basilica of St. Paul Outside the Walls, prayed on the threshold, and went forward with the Orthodox Metropolitan, the Archbishop of Canterbury, and many other representatives.

I dream of a Church that is on a *journey*, the People of God who, behind the Pope, carry the cross, enter the temple of God and, in prayer and song, encounter the Risen Christ, our one hope, Mary, and all the saints.

I dream of a Church that carries in its heart the *fire* of the Holy Spirit—and where the Spirit is, there is freedom; there is sincere dialogue with the world and especially with the young, with the poor, and with the marginalized; and there is discernment of the signs of the times. The social doctrine of the Church, the instrument of evangelization,[5] guides us in this discernment amid today's social changes.

I dream of a Church that is a concrete *witness of hope and of love*, as personified by the Pope who embraces all: Orthodox, Anglican, Calvinist, Lutheran...in the grace of Jesus Christ, in the love of the Father, and in the communion of the Spirit lived in prayer and humility.

What joy! What hope!

Maria sanctissima, vita, dulcedo et spes nostra,
ora pro nobis!

Mary most holy, our life, our sweetness, and our hope, pray for us!

---

5. Cf. John Paul II, *Centesimus Annus* (On the Hundredth Anniversary of *Rerum Novarum*). Boston: Pauline Books & Media, 1991, n. 54.

5

THE ONE THING NECESSARY

God and Not the Works of God

In this Jubilee year, John Paul II began his many pilgrimages with those places most significant in salvation history. When he was unable to travel to Ur in Chaldea, he commemorated the patriarch Abraham in Rome.

Putting aside everything at the Lord's call, Abraham chose God. He obeyed without hesitation, and without knowing where he was going, he set out from his homeland toward the land promised to him by God. The holy patriarch began his extraordinary experience with this radical choice.

Abraham "lived as a stranger in the land God had promised him."

Abraham did not doubt that God would keep his promise to give him a son even at his advanced age of 100.

"By faith Abraham, when put to the test, offered up Isaac" in sacrifice, because "he considered the fact that God was able to raise someone from the dead…" (cf. Heb 11:9–19).

Precisely in this way, Abraham became the father of a multitude of people, as numerous as the stars in the heavens and the grains of sand on the seashore.

To rely on God alone, to choose God alone. This was the great experience of the patriarchs, of the prophets, and of the first Christians as recalled in the eleventh chapter of Hebrews in which the expression *"through faith"* is repeated eighteen times, and once, the expression *"with faith."*

To not entrust oneself entirely to God means that one seeks support and security in other places. This has always been the temptation of the People of God, the experience suffered by important and even glorious people like Moses, David, Solomon....

Jesus and Mary were the *faithful ones* par excellence. And with them, a myriad of witnesses, an array of great examples has never been lacking in the history of the universal Church and in the events of our own personal lives.

The foundation of Christian life

During my long nine-year ordeal of solitary confinement, I was in a cell without windows. For days at a time the electric lights were left on both day and night; and then for days at a time there was complete darkness. I felt as though I were suffocating from the heat and humidity to the point of insanity. I was still a young bishop with only eight years of pastoral experience. I could not sleep because I was so tormented by the thought of being forced to abandon my diocese, and of the many works that I had begun for God now going to ruin. I experienced a kind of revolt in my whole being.

One night, from the depths of my heart, a voice said to me, "Why do you torment yourself like this? You must distinguish between God and the works of God. Everything you have done and desire to continue doing—pastoral visits, formation of seminarians, of men and women religious, of the laity, of the youth, construction of schools, *foyers* for students, missions for the evangelization of non-Christians—all of these are excellent works. These are God's works, but *they* are not God! If God wants you to leave all of these works, do it right away and have faith in him! God can do things infinitely better than you can. He will entrust his works to others that are much more capable. You have chosen God alone, not his works!"

This light gave me a new peace and completely changed my way of thinking. It helped me to surmount moments that were almost physically impossible to overcome. From then on, a new strength filled my heart that stayed with me for thirteen years. Feeling my human weakness, I renewed my choice of God in the face of very difficult situations, and I was never without peace.

To choose God and not the works of God. This is the foundation of the Christian life in every age. At the same time, it is the truest response to the world of today. Through it, God's plans for us, for the Church, and for humanity in our time are realized.

A "fiat" always renewed

Every day I understand more clearly the words of Sacred Scripture: "For as the heavens are higher than the earth, so are my ways higher than your ways and my thoughts than your thoughts" (Is 55:9).

I understand that each moment my life is a series of choices between God and the works of God, a choice that is always new, a choice that becomes conversion.

Mary chose God. She abandoned her projects without fully understanding the mystery that was being accomplished in her body and in her destiny. From the moment of the Annunciation, she lived a continually renewed "fiat": from the crib in Bethlehem to the exile in Egypt, from the carpenter's shop at Nazareth to Calvary. She always made the same choice, "God and not the works of God." It was precisely in this way that Mary was able to see all the promises fulfilled. She saw her lifeless Son, whom she had held in her arms, rise from the dead. She saw the group of disciples compose themselves again and begin to announce her Son's Gospel to all peoples. She would be proclaimed blessed and

"Mother of God" by all generations, she who, beneath the cross, received a simple man as her son in the place of her divine Son.

True worship

"You shall love the Lord your God with all your heart, and with all your soul, and with all your might" (Deut 6:5; cf. Mt 22:37).

In the books of Leviticus and Deuteronomy, God meticulously established the ceremonies, the prayers, the priestly vestments, and all other things necessary for official worship according to different times, feasts, and solemnities.

The Second Book of Kings tells us of the great deeds accomplished by Solomon in building up the Temple in accordance with the plan established by God, with the contribution of the neighboring peoples. Thus was born the religious and national center of Israel.

Nevertheless, God, through the prophets, has taught us that sacrifices and holocausts mean nothing if there is not the interior sacrifice of a contrite and humble heart, an authentic choice that is clearly known to God. The heavens are his and the earth is his "footstool." God does not need a Temple (cf. Is 66:1–2).

The courage of consistency

This choice of God in our life has, as a necessary consequence, the categorical rejection of idolatry. So it was that the ancient Eleazar preferred to die rather than make others doubtful of his total adhesion to God (cf. 2 Mac 6:18–31).

Today, as in the time of the Old and New Testaments, one who chooses God must accept possible disadvantages—in the economic area, in power, or in other interests—as Jesus said, "because of me..." (Mt 10:22). Because of this choice, many people cannot enter a university, obtain employment, or find housing.... Generations of Christians in many countries have courageously accepted these sacrifices.

> Recall the earlier days of your faith! After you were enlightened, you stood firm through a hard struggle which involved suffering. At times you were publicly insulted and mistreated, while at other times you stood by those who were so treated. You shared the sufferings of prisoners and accepted the seizure of your possessions with joy, because you knew you had a better and more permanent possession (Heb 10:32–34).

The choice of God in a pastor's life

When I was in prison, in a certain sense it was easier to make a choice for God alone. The temptations to descend into compromises were not lacking, but it was truly when every former security fell away that I felt I must concentrate all my life on the "one thing necessary" (cf. Lk 10:42), on what is solely important.

Now that I am free and immersed in my work and at times with grave commitments, it is much easier to be a Martha than a Mary.

Every pastor, in fact, believes he has chosen God alone. We lavish great dedication on God's works, but I always feel I must sincerely examine myself again before him. In my pastoral life, how much is for him and how much is for his works (which at times may actually be my own works)? In refusing to leave an assignment or in desiring another, am I really disinterested?

The author of the Letter to the Hebrews gives this advice: "For you need endurance" (Heb 10:36). Endurance is needed in order to be truly free. Like Moses, one who is free has no fear: "Through faith Moses, when he had grown up, refused to be called a son of Pharaoh's daughter, choosing to suffer with God's people rather than enjoy the transitory pleasures of sin" (Heb 11:24–25).

The magnetic strength of witness

During a recent conference at the University of Salford in Great Britain, a seminarian who spoke in the name of his fellow seminarians asked, "Father, can you leave us some advice?" I answered, "Your request takes me by surprise, but I don't want to leave you disappointed. In my already long life and travels, I have had this experience: if I follow Jesus faithfully, step by step, he will bring me to my goal. Walk on unforeseeable paths, at times tortuous, obscure, and dramatic, but be faithful—you are with Jesus! Cast all your cares and worries on him. Don't worry about how you will attract the crowd; be certain that if you follow Jesus, the people will follow you!"

In the *Acts of the Martyrs* we read this account of the life of St. Cyprian. When he was arrested, the magistrate interrogated him before a crowd.

"Are you Thascius Cyprianus?"

"I am."

"Our most venerable emperors have commanded you to sacrifice."

"I will not do it."

"Reconsider!"

"In so just a cause there is no need for any deliberation."

"It is decided that Thascius Cyprianus should die by the sword."

"Thanks be to God."

Cyprian's choice was like a magnetic force, and he made this choice so that his faithful would follow him as one to the place of martyrdom.[1]

I think of the Jubilee pilgrimage. Let us make progress every day, in spite of trials and risks, because we have one goal, we have one hope.

Porro unum est necessariu.

One thing only is necessary.

---

1. Cf. *Acta Proconsularia St. Cyprian*, 3–4: PL 3, 1561–1563.

THE ADVENTURE OF HOPE

6

WHETHER WE EAT, WHETHER WE DRINK
The Present Moment

Through a strange alienation, man in this world lives in the past, in his memories, or in expectation of the future, while he seeks to avoid the present moment, or exercises his spirit in inventing ways to "kill time." This kind of person does not live in the here and now, but in a fantasy of which he is unaware.... The past and the future, in their abstract dislocation, are non-existent, and have no access to eternity; eternity only touches the present moment and only gives itself to someone who is totally present in that moment. It is only in these instants that one may reach and live in the image of the eternal present.[1]

I would like to consider the present moment with you in this meditation. It is in the present that our adventure of hope begins. This is the only time we have in our hands. The past is already gone, and we do not know if there will be a future. The present moment is our great wealth.

To live for the present is a rule of our times. In the frenetic rhythms of our era, we must stop in the present moment as our only chance to really "live" and to set our earthly life now on the course to life eternal.

---

1. P. Evdokimov, *Le Eta della Vita Spirituale*. Bologna: 1968, pp. 257–258.

The way to holiness

After my arrest in August of 1975, I was taken during the night from Saigon to Nha Trang. I made that 450-kilometer journey between two policemen. Thus, I began the life of a prisoner; I no longer had a schedule. I experienced the truth of the Vietnamese proverb that says, "One day in prison is worth a thousand autumns in freedom." In prison, everyone waits for freedom every day, every minute of every day.

During those days and months, my mind was racked with many confused feelings: sadness, fear, tension…. The great distance that lay between my people and me broke my heart. In the darkness of this terrible night, in the middle of an ocean of anguish, I slowly woke up. "I have to face reality," I told myself. "I am in prison. If I wait for the opportune moment to do something really great, how many times will such occasions actually present themselves? Only one thing comes with certainty: death. I have to take advantage of the occasions that present themselves every day. I have to accomplish ordinary actions in an extraordinary way."

I was convinced during the long nights in prison that living the present moment is the most simple and most secure way to holiness. From this conviction a prayer was born:

Jesus, I will not wait; I will live the present moment
    and fill it with love.
A straight line is made of millions of little points,
    one united with the other.
My life, too, is made of millions of seconds and minutes
    united one with the other.
If I arrange every single point perfectly, the line will be
    straight.
If I live every minute perfectly, my life will be holy.
The road of hope is paved with little steps of hope.
The life of hope is made of brief minutes of hope.

As you, Jesus, always did what pleased your Father,
   every minute I want to say: Jesus, I love you,
and my life is always a "new and eternal covenant"
   with you.
Every minute I want to sing with the whole Church:
Glory to the Father and to the Son and to the Holy
   Spirit....

Duties and gifts

In the Gospel, Jesus always exhorts us to live in the
present moment. He has us ask our Father for our bread, but
just for "today's," and reminds us that there are enough worries for "every day" (cf. Mt 6:34).

Jesus challenges us each second, and at the same time, he
gives us everything. To the thief on the cross who said,
"Jesus, remember me when you come into your kingdom,"
Jesus responded, "Today you will be with me in paradise" (cf.
Lk 23:42–43). In this word "today" lies all the forgiveness
and love of Jesus.

St. Paul stresses to the maximum this identification with
Jesus in every moment, to the point of creating a new and
much more expressive terminology:

- *"confixus cruci,"* I have been crucified with Christ
  (Gal 2:20);
- *"consepulti,"* we have been buried with him (Rom 6:4;
  Col 2:12);
- *"conmortui sumus," "convivemus,"* to die together and
  to live together (2 Tim 2:8; 2 Cor 7:3);
- *"consurrexistis,"* to rise with him (Col 3:1).

The Apostle speaks of Jesus' union with us as an unfailing reality, a life that is unbroken, which engages our whole
being and awaits our response. Christ has died and has come

back to life to be Lord of both the living and the dead. Because of this, "whether we live or whether we die, we are the Lord's" (Rom 14:8–9). "So whether you eat or drink, or whatever you do, do everything for the glory of God" (1 Cor 10:31).

In the fourth Gospel, this christological dimension opens to us the trinitarian dimension: "So that they may be one, as we are one. I in them and you in me" (Jn 17:22–23).

In the present: the heart of God

All of the saints and great witnesses agree on the importance of living the present moment well. They lived united to Jesus in each moment of their lives according to an ideal that they incarnated in their very being. For Ignatius of Loyola it was, "*Ad maiorem Dei gloriam,*" to the greater glory of God; for Elizabeth of the Trinity, "*In laudem gloriae,*" to praise his glory; for John Bosco, "*Da mihi animas,*" give me souls; for Mother Teresa, "*misericordia,*" mercy; for Raul Follereau, "*Jesus in the lepers*"; and for Jean Vanier it is, "*Jesus in the mentally handicapped.*"

Personifying their ideals in the present moment, the saints realized these ideals in their very essence.

St. Paul of the Cross writes:

Happy the soul who reposes in the bosom of God *(in sinu Dei),* without thinking of the future, but managing to live moment by moment in him, without any other preoccupation than doing well his will in every event.[2]

St. Therese of the Child Jesus also affirms this:

My life is but an instant, a passing hour.
My life is but a day that escapes and flies away.

---

2. St. Paul of the Cross, *Lettere*, I. Rome: 1924, pp. 645–646.

O my God! You know that to love you on this earth,
I only have today![3]

And a great spiritual figure of our time says:

One who knows the way of holiness turns and returns
passionately to the asceticism that it requires: to live in
God in the present moment of life. In this way, one is
completely detached from all that is not God, and is immersed in God wherever he is. So then, our life is no
longer "to exist," but completely "to be," because God,
he who is, *is* in it.[4]

Discerning the voice of God

Discerning the voice of God among the many inner voices
(cf. *Gaudium et Spes,* n. 16) so as to accomplish his will in the
present moment is an ongoing exercise that the saints under-
took willingly. With continual exercise, discernment becomes
always easier because the voice of God within us grows
louder and stronger. But at times it is not easy. Still, if we
believe in God's love, then we can do what we believe to be
God's will with security, trusting that if it is not, he will set us
back on the right way. "Now we know that God works in
every way for the good with those who love him and are
called in accordance with his plan," Paul reminds the Romans
(8:28).

Origen leaves us this beautiful advice:

We do not need to look in a place for the sanctuary, but
in deeds, in life, and in customs. If these are according
to God, if they conform to the commandments of God, it

---

3. St. Therese of Lisieux, *The Poetry of Saint Therese of Lisieux*. Trans.
by Donald Kinney, O.C.D. Washington, D.C.: ICS Publications, 1996,
p. 51.

4. Chiara Lubich, *Scritti Spirituali, 2*. Rome: 1984, p. 129.

matters little whether you are at home or in the public square…what am I saying, "in the public square"? It does not even matter if you find yourself in the theater—if you are serving the Word of God, you are in the sanctuary, have no doubt.[5]

And Raissa Maritain writes: "Beneath obscure appearances of the duties of every moment hides the divine will; these are like sacraments of the present moment."[6]

How to fill up each moment with love

When under house arrest in the village of Cây Vông, I was under police surveillance day and night, and this thought became obsessive: "My people! My people that I love so much; a flock without a shepherd! How can I contact my people at a time when they have most need of their pastor? The Catholic bookstores have been confiscated, the schools closed, the religious dispersed. Some have gone to work in the rice camps and others find themselves in the 'region of the new economy' in the midst of the general population, in the villages. This separation is a shock that destroys my heart."

I told myself, "I will not wait. I want to live the present moment, filling it with love, but how?"

One night a light came to me: "Francis, it is very simple. Do as St. Paul did when he was in prison. Write letters to the different communities."

The following morning while it was still dark, I signaled to Quang, a seven-year-old boy who returned from Mass at 5:00 A.M. I said to him: "Tell your mother to buy old calendars for me." That night, once more in the dark, Quang brought me the calendars. Every single day in October and November of

---

5. *Omelia sul Levitico* 12, 4: SC 287, 182.
6. *Diario de Raissa,* courtesy of J. Maritain. Brescia: 1968, p. 146.

1975, I wrote messages to my people from prison. Each morning Quang came to take the papers and bring them home so that his brothers and sisters could recopy the messages. That is how the book, *The Road of Hope*, came to be written and has since been published in eleven languages.

When I was finally released from prison in 1989, I received a letter from Mother Teresa. It contained these words: "It is not the number of our works that are important, but the intensity of the love that we put into every action."

The moment that will be the last

To live each moment intensely is also the secret of knowing how to live our last moment well. Paul VI wrote in his "Thoughts on Death":

I will no longer look back, but do willingly, simply, humbly, and bravely the duties that come from the circumstances in which I find myself, as your will. To do quickly. To do everything. To do it well. To do it joyfully—whatever you want of me right now, even if it is beyond my strength, even if it asks my life. Finally, at this last hour.[7]

Every word, every gesture, every telephone call, every decision we make should be the most beautiful one of our life, giving our love and our smile to everyone, without losing a second.

Let every moment of our life be
    the first moment,
    the last moment,
    the only moment.

---

7. Paul VI, *Pensiero alla Morte. L'Osservatore Romano,* Aug. 5, 1979, p. 5.

I would like to conclude this meditation with a prayer of St. Faustina Kowalska:

If I look at the future, I am full of fear,
but why go forward into the future?
Only the present moment is dear to me,
because perhaps the future will not lodge in my soul.

The past is not within my power
to change, correct, or add something.
Neither the wise nor the prophets were able to do this.
I trust therefore to God that which regards my past.

O present moment, you belong to me completely;
I desire to use you as much as it is within my power....

Therefore, trusting in your mercy,
I go forward in life as a child,
and every day I offer to you my heart
enflamed with love for your greater glory.[8]

---

8. St. Faustina Kowalska, *Davanti a Lui: Pagine dal Diario*. Milan: 1999, pp. 31–32.

7

My Words Are Spirit and Life
To Be Word

When I was a student in the minor seminary in Annin, a Vietnamese priest and professor helped me to understand the importance of having the Gospel with me always. He was an intellectual, of mandarin descent, and a convert from Buddhism. He always carried the New Testament with him, hanging it from his neck as you would Viaticum. When I left the seminary for another assignment, he gave me this book, his most precious treasure, as a heritage.

The example of this holy priest, Joseph Maria Thich, always remained alive in my heart and helped me immensely in prison during my time in solitary confinement. I kept going during those difficult years because the Word of God was "a lamp for my feet" and a "light for my way" (cf. Ps 119:105).

St. Jerome and St. Therese of the Child Jesus always carried the Gospel close to their hearts. But it is my own culture that emphasizes the unique value of the Scriptures. In Asia the words of Confucius and Mencius, his disciple, are greatly venerated. Since the people cannot keep the words everywhere, they keep them in their minds as a sign of their veneration.

The Word and the words

When Jesus manifested his glory to Peter, James, and John in the Transfiguration, a voice was heard from the clouds saying, "This is my Son, the Beloved, listen to him" (Lk 9:35).

The words of Jesus are not like the words of men, and his first listeners were immediately aware of this fact, for "he was teaching them on his own authority, and not like their scribes" (Mt 7:29).

It is not by chance that the Gospel exercises a great fascination even beyond the Christian world. Mahatma Gandhi, for example, left these words:

> When I read the Gospel and arrived at the Sermon on the Mount, I began to profoundly accept the Christian teaching. The teaching of the Sermon on the Mount re-echoed within me something I had grasped in my childhood, something that seemed to be proper to my being, and that I seemed to see actualized in my everyday life…. Profoundly refresh yourself at the fountain of the Sermon on the Mount.[1]

The fact is, the words of Jesus possess a substance and depth that other words do not, whether they be philosophical, political, or poetic. The words of Jesus are, as often defined in the New Testament, "words of life." They contain, express, and communicate a life, and even more, "eternal life," the fullness of life.

I love the sixth chapter of the Gospel of John. Jesus' revelation of the bread of life made the way of discipleship more arduous, and at that moment, many of the disciples left. Then Jesus asked the twelve, "Do you also wish to go away?"

---

1. *Buddhism, Christianity, and Islam. Tascabili Economici.* Newton, 1993, p. 52.

Peter answers, "Lord, to whom can we go? You have the words of eternal life" (cf. Jn 6:67–68).

All the strength and frailty of our hope depends on these words.

Word and Eucharist, one table

From the first pages of Sacred Scripture, we see that the Word of God is uniquely efficacious. "God spoke," we read in the book of Genesis, "and light was." "God spoke...and so it came to be" (cf. Gen 1:3, 7, 11, 15, 24, 30). After the fall of our first parents, the Word of God restored the hope of salvation with the promise of redemption (cf. Gen 3:15). With the call of Abraham, God made a people for himself. God shapes history with his words, speaking to the patriarchs and communicating his promises to them. He tells Moses to liberate his chosen people from their slavery in Egypt. He transmits words of truth through the prophets in expectation of the future Messiah, the one Savior.

Jesus, however, is the Word par excellence. "Jesus Christ, therefore, the Word made flesh, was sent as 'a man among men,'[2]" affirms *Dei Verbum*. "He 'speaks the words of God' (cf. Jn 3:34) and completes the work of salvation which his Father gave him to do (cf. Jn 5:36; 17:4)" (n. 4).

To understand the importance of the Word of God for the Church, there is no clearer image than the attitude of the Church. For two thousand years, the Church "has always venerated the divine Scriptures just as she venerates the Body of the Lord, since, especially in the sacred liturgy, she unceasingly receives and offers to the faithful the bread of life from the table both of God's Word and of Christ's Body" (*Dei Verbum*, n. 21).

---

2. *Epist. Ad Diognetum*, 7, 4: Funk, *Patres Apostolici*, I, p. 403.

Throughout the whole of Christian tradition, this connection between the Word and the Eucharist—both the nourishment of Christianity—is constantly recurring. "We drink the blood of Christ," writes Origen, "not only when we receive it according to the rites of the mysteries, but also when we receive his words in which resides life."[3] St. Jerome says that "The knowledge of Scripture is truly food and drink that is received in the Word of God."[4] From St. Ambrose we read: "If we drink the blood of Christ by which we are redeemed, as we drink the words of the Scripture, these pass within our veins and, assimilated, enter into our life."[5]

Again, St. Jerome affirms:

> I hold that the Gospel is the body of Jesus and the Scriptures are his teachings. The words of Jesus: "One who eats my body and drinks my blood" (Jn 6:54), can be understood to mean the mystery (Eucharistic) and also, as that true body and blood of Christ that is the word of Scripture.... The Word of God is that flesh and that blood of Christ that enters within us through listening.[6]

The bread of the Word, as *Dei Verbum* reminds us, is nourishment that instills vigor, enlightens the mind, strengthens the will, re-enkindles the heart, and renews life (cf. n. 23).

I would like to speak of my own experience on this theme.

When I had lost everything and was in prison, I thought to prepare myself a "vademecum," a small collection of Scripture verses that would enable me to live the Word of God even in that situation. I had neither paper nor notebook. But the police supplied me with some sheets of paper that I was supposed to use to respond to all their questions. So, little by little, I began to set aside some pieces of paper, and I man-

---

3. *In Numeros Homilia,* 61, 9: PG 12, 701.

4. *Commentarius in Ecclesiastem,* III, 8, 12–13: CCL 72, 278.

5. *Enarrationes in XXI Psalmos Davidicos,* Psalm 1, 33: PL 14, 984.

6. Cf. *Breviarium in Psalmos,* Psalm 147: PL 26, 1334.

aged to make a tiny notebook. Day by day, I was able to write in Latin the more than 300 sentences of Sacred Scripture that I recalled from memory. The Word of God, thus reconstructed, was my daily vademecum, my precious jewel-case from which I drew strength and nourishment.

To accept and to live the Word of God

Because the Word gives life and brings with it all its fruits, it is necessary to both accept and to live the Word.

The principal attitude required before the Word of God that speaks and communicates itself is that of listening and accepting. "Listen to him" is exactly the command the Father addresses to the disciples regarding his Son. This is a listening more of the heart than of the ears. The word, in fact, bears fruit only if it finds fertile soil, that is, when it falls into a "good and perfect heart" (cf. Lk 8:15).

But it is not enough only to meditate on the Word of God, not enough to penetrate it with the mind, to pray with it, to draw some considerations or proposals from it. Authentic listening to the Word is translated into obedience, into doing what the Word demands of us. We must allow ourselves to work by the Word, until we arrive at the point that it animates our entire Christian life. We must apply the Word to all the circumstances of our existence and transform it into life, as St. James admonishes, "But be doers of the Word and not merely hearers" (Jas 1:22).

Acquiring the mind of Christ

In prison I wrote, "Obey only one rule: the Gospel. This constitution is superior to all others. It is the rule that Jesus left to his apostles (cf. Mt 4:23). It is not difficult, complicated, or legalistic like the others. On the contrary, it is dynamic, kind, and invigorating for your soul. A saint who is far from the Gospel is a false saint."[7]

In fact, by entering us the Word of God questions our human ways of thinking and acting, and it introduces us to the new style of life inaugurated by Christ. For those who live the Gospel, it is possible to arrive, with Paul, at having "the mind of Christ" (cf. 1 Cor 2:16). It is also possible to acquire the capacity to read the signs of the times with the gaze of Christ himself and, therefore, to creatively affect history; to experience true freedom, joy, and the courage of evangelical consistency; to find new faith in the Father with the rapport of authentic and sincere children; and to have a concrete and effective attitude of service toward all people.

The Gospel, in short, awakens in us a profound sense of our life—we know finally why we are alive, and it makes us hope anew.

The result is that it is no longer we who live, but Christ who comes to live in us. Through the words of Scripture, the Word makes his home in us and transforms us into *verba nel Verbo,* "word into the Word."

"How does Jesus make himself present in the soul?" asked Paul VI. And he answered, "Through the vehicle of the communication of word proceeds the divine thought, the Word, the Son of God made man. One could assert that the Lord incarnates himself in us when we allow his Word to come to live in us."[8]

Communicating the Word

It is not enough to accept and to live the Word. It must also be shared. We do this through catechesis, homilies, and

---

7. Francis X. Nguyễn Văn Thuận, *The Road of Hope.* Rome: 1992, p. 194 (n. 985).

8. *Teachings of Paul VI,* V (1967). Cittá del Vaticano: 1968, p. 936.

in the preaching of spiritual exercises. What we might not always do is to give the fruit of the Word.

The Word is a seed sown in our life. Good soil does not give back the seed, but the fruit. We must not communicate only our reflections on the Word of God, but above all, what the Word has done once it has been accepted into the soil of our life. Is it not true that witnesses are more credible than teachers are, unless they are also witnesses?

Such a sharing of the Word allows us also to glimpse what is the typical Christian announcement: to communicate a life (*the* Life), and, therefore, to witness to an experience. This was well understood by the Johannine community: "What was from the beginning, what we have heard, what we have seen with our eyes, what we have looked at and touched with our hands...we also proclaim to you so you too may have fellowship with us" (1 Jn 1:1–3).

Only in this way does the Reign of God advance, and true communion expands to the point of accepting all humanity in the unity of the Father, of the Son, and of the Holy Spirit.

The Catholics in the prison of Phú Khánh had secretly brought in a copy of the New Testament. They divided the book into small pieces and distributed these pieces among the Catholics who began to learn the passages by heart. Since the cells had floors of sand, when they heard a guard's footsteps, they would hide the Word of God by burying it in the floor.

In the darkness of night, the prisoners would recite in turn the part of the New Testament each had already memorized. It was an impressive and moving experience to hear the Word of God proclaimed in the silence and darkness of the prison. To be in the presence of Jesus the "living Gospel" spoken by the prisoners with all the strength of soul; to hear the priestly prayer and the passion of Christ....

The non-Christians also listened with respect and admiration to what they called the "Sacred Word." Many said they felt the Word of God to be "spirit and life."

With only the Gospel

I have always prayed to St. Joseph to help me put the Gospel into practice. Although he was the foster father of Jesus, he never received a sacrament in his life (the sacraments were not yet instituted). He lived with the Word, listened to it, accepted it, put it into practice, communicated and shared it—so much so that his carpenter's shop became a school of the Gospel. For this reason I consider St. Joseph a patron of all those who live the Word.

I would like to conclude this meditation by directing our gaze on ourselves, we who collaborate with the Holy Father in his petrine ministry. Many times I ask myself how I can accomplish a change of mentality, a constant re-evangelization of life, and an authentic conversion during this Jubilee Year?

When the Holy Father went through the Holy Door with only the Gospel, I learned a great lesson. *Here* is the way, *here* is the icon of the Roman Curia for the Third Millennium—a Church that welcomes, lives, shares, and announces the Gospel of hope.

8

The Bond of Perfection
The Art of Loving

In preparing for this meditation, I felt the words of Paul resounding within me, "If I do not have love, I am nothing" (1 Cor 13:2). These words recall me to the work of conversion, and I remember that "above all" (cf. 1 Pet 4:8), even before preaching or praying or any other apostolic service whatsoever, I must have love. Even more, I have to *be* love.

Without love, I do not possess God and I cannot give him to others. I do not even know him (cf. 1 Jn 4:5). If I write meditations, if I conduct the spiritual exercises for important people, if "I give my body over to be burned" (1 Cor 13:3), or if I remain in a prison for long years, but I do not have love— and God is love—it is all a waste of energy, as Augustine would say.[1]

The world belongs to the one who loves it

At times we complain that Christianity in today's world is always more marginalized, that it has become difficult to pass on the faith to the young, and that vocations are diminishing. One could continue listing reasons for worry....

Not infrequently in fact, we feel ourselves lost in today's world, but the adventure of hope brings us beyond that. One day I found these words written on a calendar, "The world

---

1. Cf. *Defensor Grammaticus, Liber Scintillarum*: SC 77, 58.

belongs to those who love it and to those who know how to prove it." How true these words are! In the heart of every person there is an infinite thirst for love, and with the love which God has placed in our hearts (cf. Rom 5:5) we can satisfy that thirst.

However, it is necessary that our love be an "art," an art that exceeds the ability to love in a merely human way. Much, if not all, depends on this art.

I have seen this art lived, for example, by Mother Teresa of Calcutta. Whoever met her loved her. Likewise, Pope John XXIII, now proclaimed a Blessed, knew this art and, many years after his death, his memory is still alive among the people.

When entering a convent or a diocesan office, or even our own offices, one does not always find this art, which makes Christianity a beautiful and attractive force. Instead, one finds faces that appear sad or annoyed by everyday *routine*. Will not the lack of vocations depend on this? And on the feeble effect of our witness? Without a strong love, we cannot give witness to hope!

Although we are experts in religion, we always run the risk of possessing a theory of love but not enough of the art of love. As a doctor who has the knowledge but not the art of healing, people may consult him when they are sick, but when they are better they never go back.

Jesus, as no other, was a master in the art of loving. An immigrant to a strange land always brings—at least in his heart—the laws and customs of his own people even while adapting to his new surroundings. So Jesus, on coming to earth as a pilgrim of the Trinity, brought the way of life from his heavenly homeland, "expressing humanly the divine ways of the Trinity."[2]

---

2. Cf. *Catechism of the Catholic Church*, n. 470.

Distinctions of Christian love

Let us contemplate together then, the distinctive elements of the art of love that Jesus teaches and that are the source of splendor and fascination of the Christian life.

1. Love first

The love of God that Jesus has sown in our hearts with the gift of the Holy Spirit is a completely gratuitous love. This is a love without self-interest, without expecting anything in return. This love does not give love only when it is loved, or for any other motive however good, such as human friendship. It does not stop to discover if the other is friendly or hostile, but loves first and takes the initiative.

While we were still ungrateful and indifferent sinners, Christ died for us (cf. Rom 5:8). "He loved us first," says John (1 Jn 4:19), and we should do likewise. "Do not wait to be loved by another, but make headway and begin," recommends St. John Chrysostom.[3]

2. Love everyone

To make God's love shine brightly, we have to love everyone and exclude no one. Jesus tells us: "Be children of your Father in heaven; for he makes his sun rise on the good and the evil..." (Mt 5:45). We are called to be small suns next to the Sun of the Love who is God. Thus, everyone is the object of our love. Everyone! Not an ideal "everyone" of all those people in the world we will probably never meet, but a concrete "everyone."

"To love a person, we have to meet him or her," says Mother Teresa. "I never take care of crowds, only persons."[4]

---

3. *In Ep. Ad Rom. Hom.*, 21, 2: PG 60, 605.
4. Mother Teresa of Calcutta, *Tu Mi Porti L'Amore*. Rome: 1979, p. 48.

"As one consecrated host is enough, among the billions of hosts on earth, to nourish ourselves with God," assures Chiara Lubich, "one brother is enough—he whom the will of God puts before us—to place us in communication with the humanity that is the mystical Jesus."[5]

Every neighbor gives me the possibility of loving Christ who, "with the Incarnation…is united in a certain way with every man" (*Gaudium et Spes,* n. 22).

3. Love enemies

A unique characteristic of Christian love is the love of enemies, an aspect that non-believers find inconceivable. One day in prison I was asked:

"Do you love us?"

"Yes, I love you."

"But we have kept you in prison for so many years, without a trial, without a sentence, and you love us? That's impossible! Perhaps it's not true!"

"I've been with you many years, you've seen it's true."

"When you are free, won't you send your faithful to burn our homes, to kill our families?"

"No! Even if you want to kill me, I love you."

"But why?"

"Because Jesus has taught me to love everyone, even my enemies. If I don't, I am no longer worthy to be called a Christian."

"It's very beautiful, but very hard to understand."

Jesus insisted on this mark of Christian love, and only with this attitude of heart can one bring true peace to the earth. "For if you love those who love you…and if you greet only your brothers and sisters…. Do not even the Gentiles also do the same?… But I say to you, love your enemies and pray for those who persecute you" (Mt 5:46–47, 44).

---

5. C. Lubich, *Scritti Spirituali 1*. Rome: 1997, p. 33.

4. Love by giving your life

Jesus is God, and like God's love, his is infinite. It is not a love that gives some*thing,* but that gives himself: "Having loved his own…he loved them to the end" (Jn 13:1). "Greater love than this no man has—to lay down his life for his friends" (Jn 15:13).

Jesus gave all and without reserve. He gave his life on the cross and he gave his body and blood in the Eucharist. Even we are called to this measure of love: to be ready to give our life for those who work with us; ready to give our life for one another.

5. Love in service

For the greater majority, this "giving of one's life" that Jesus speaks of is not accomplished through blood. It is achieved in the many small actions of everyday life, in putting ourselves at the service of others, including those whom, for whatever reason, might seem "inferior" to us.

In recounting the solemn hour of the Last Supper, the evangelist John does not speak of the institution of the Eucharist as do the Synoptic Gospels. Rather, he speaks of Jesus who washes the feet of his disciples "that you also should do as I have done to you" (Jn 13:15).

To serve means to become "eucharist" for others, to identify ourselves with them, to share their joys and sorrows (cf. Rom 12:15), to learn to think with their heads, to feel with their hearts, to live their lives, "to walk in their moccasins," as an Indian proverb says.

Love: the first evangelization

I remember moments in my life that continue to be a light for me today when I think of the great duty of Christian witness.

When I was in isolation, five police took turns so that there were always two guarding me. The leaders had told them, "We will replace you every two weeks with another group so that you will not be 'contaminated' by this danger- ous bishop."

Afterward the leaders told them, "We've decided not to switch you anymore; otherwise this bishop will contaminate all of the police."

In the beginning, the guards did not talk to me. They only answered me with a yes or no. I was terribly sad. I wanted to be kind and polite with them, but it was impossible. They avoided speaking with me.

One night a thought came to me: "Francis, you are still very rich. You have the love of Christ in your heart; love them as Jesus has loved you."

The next day I started to love them even more, to love Jesus in them, smiling and exchanging kind words with them. I began to tell stories of my trips abroad, of how people live in America, in Canada, in Japan, in the Philippines…about eco- nomics, about freedom, about technology.

This stimulated their curiosity and they began asking me many questions. Little by little we became friends. They wanted to learn foreign languages, French, English…. And my guards became my students!

On another occasion, on the mountain of Vĩnh Phú and in the prison of Vĩnh Quảng, I had to cut wood on a rainy day. I spoke to the guard.

"Can I ask you a favor?"

"Tell me. I'll help you."

"I would like to cut a piece of wood in the shape of a cross."

"Don't you know it's severely forbidden to have any religious signs whatsoever?"

"I know," I answered, "but we are friends, and I promise to keep it hidden."

"It will be really dangerous for us."

"Close your eyes. I'll do it now and I'll be really careful."

He went away and left me alone. I cut the cross and kept it hidden in a piece of soap—up until the time of my release. This piece of wood, later placed within a metal frame, became my pectoral cross.

In another prison I asked my guard, who had become my friend, for a piece of electrical wire. Frightened, he said to me:

"I learned at the Police Academy that when someone asks for electrical wire it means they want to kill themselves!"

I explained to him, "Catholic priests don't commit suicide."

"But what do you want to do with electrical wire?"

"I would like to make a chain to carry my cross."

"How can you make a chain with electrical wire? It's impossible!"

"If you bring me two small pincers, I'll show you."

"It's too dangerous!"

"But we're friends!"

Three days later he said to me: "It's really hard to refuse you anything. Tomorrow night, when it's my shift, I will bring you a piece of electrical wire. But you have to finish everything in four hours."

The next evening from 7:00 to 11:00, with two little pincers we cut the electrical wire into pieces the size of match sticks. We put them together…and the chain was ready by the time the next guard came on duty.

I carry this cross and chain with me every day, not because they are remembrances of the prison, but because they represent my profound conviction. They constantly remind me that only Christian love can change hearts, not weapons, not threats, and not the media.

It is love that prepares the way for the announcement of the Gospel.

Omnia vincit amor, "love conquers everything!"

When love is true, it stirs a response of greater love. Then a person loves and is loved in return, and the new commandment of Jesus, "Love one another as I have loved you" (Jn 15:12), is realized. Reciprocal love is the fulfillment of the art of loving.

The Mother of Fair Love

We cannot conclude this meditation without turning our minds and hearts to the Blessed Mother. Mary is like the moon reflecting all the beauty of the sun that is Jesus, all his feelings and, in particular, his love. Outside of the Holy Trinity, one does not find a love of God and of all humanity equal to Mary's love. She is the Mother of Fair Love. For this reason, she is beloved by the Christian people and by many non-Christians as well. We cannot love better than by uniting ourselves to the beautiful and tender love of the Virgin Mary, who possesses the most exquisite art of loving.

The art of loving is to love Jesus (because he *is* love).

The art of loving is to love as Mary loves.

The art of loving is to love like St. Therese of the Child Jesus who said: "In the heart of the Church I will be love."[6]

---

6. *Manuscrit Autobiographique,* B, 3 v, in: *Oeuvres Complètes.* Paris: 1996, p. 226.

9

Outside the Walls—All to All

All Are the People of God Entrusted to Me

At 9:00 in the evening of December 1, 1976, I suddenly found myself with a large group of prisoners. Chained one to the other in pairs, we were loaded by police onto a truck. A short trip brought us to Tân Cảng (Newport), a new military port opened by the Americans a few years before. In front of us we saw a ship, but it was hidden in such a way that people would not be aware of what was happening. We boarded and went north—a voyage of 1,700 kilometers.

Along with the other prisoners, I was taken to the hold of the ship where the coal is loaded. Our only light came from a small oil lamp; other than that, complete darkness reigned. A total of 1,500 people were forced to endure indescribable conditions. A tempest was raging in my mind. Until that night, I had at least been imprisoned within my diocese, but now I was going to who knew where! I meditated on the words of Paul: "I am on my way to Jerusalem, not knowing what will befall me there, except that the Holy Spirit testifies to me in every city that chains and suffering await me" (Acts 20:22–23). I spent that night in terrible anguish.

At the roots of evangelization

The next morning, a little sunlight infiltrated the hold of the ship and, in that funereal atmosphere I could make out the distraught and despairing faces of the prisoners around me. Some of the prisoners called for me because a man had tried to hang himself with a steel wire. I spoke with him, and in the end he accepted my counsel. (Two years ago at an interreligious encounter in California, I met this man again. Full of joy he came toward me, thanked me, and began to recount the whole incident while showing everyone the scar that still remains around his neck.)

During that trip, as the prisoners learned that Bishop Văn Thuận was on board the ship, they approached me to tell me of their anguish. The hours passed, and I found myself sharing in their sufferings and comforting them throughout the day. The second night, in the cold of that December on the Pacific Ocean, I began to understand that a new stage in my vocation was beginning. I spent that three-day journey sustaining my fellow prisoners and meditating on the passion of Jesus. I had organized various initiatives in the diocese for the evangelization of the non-Christians, but now I seemed to be following Jesus to the roots of evangelization. It was like going with him to die *extra muros*, "outside the walls"— outside the sacred wall.

Jesus crucified was present where all the accursed lived

In this meditation I would like to consider a shocking phrase from Paul: "Cursed is everyone who hangs on a tree" (Gal 3:13). This terrible statement comes from the Book of Deuteronomy. In the time of Jesus, it was accepted as a divine curse against any Hebrew who, in the name of God and in the name of the Law of Moses, underwent the Roman torture of crucifixion.

Saul was convinced of the truth of this concerning Jesus crucified. This man from Nazareth must be cursed and rejected by God. He had led the people astray; he ate with sinners, broke the laws concerning cleanliness, and pretended to be the Messiah. His death on the cross was clearly an indication that he had not acted according to the will of Yahweh.

A rabbi from his youth, Saul could not tolerate how, even after his death, the people still followed this false prophet. They created disorder in the synagogues by proclaiming Jesus as the Messiah and by claiming that he lived at the right hand of God. Saul zealously persecuted the disciples of Jesus until one day the Risen One swept him away and changed him forever. The very person Saul believed was in complete contradiction to the divine will, who was rejected by God, now strikingly revealed himself as the Son of God, as the One who makes the divine will of the Father most visible.

From then on, the curse of Deuteronomy, which at first legitimized the holy hatred toward Christians, instead revealed God's limitless love for humanity. If this Crucified One was truly the Son of God, and if, therefore, God himself was present in that man who had hung on the cross, then this death by crucifixion was no longer a curse. Rather, this death showed the extent to which God had drawn close to those who were far from him. Hanging from the cross, Jesus made himself present where all the cursed lived, there where the sinful world lived far from God. Precisely in this way, he offered reconciliation and salvation to all.

Outside the walls

The tradition of the early Church recognized this reality in another fact. Jesus died *extra muros,* "outside the city gates," as the Letter to the Hebrews says (13:12 ff.); he died outside the vineyard, that is, outside the community of Israel (cf. Lk 20:15). This means that Jesus died outside the holy place that is the presence of Yahweh, the place where only a religious man could remain. Thus, it is revealed that the love of God is encountered precisely where, in the eyes of men and women, God is not.

Going back to the fourth Song of the Servant of Yahweh (he was "counted among the impious," Is 53:12), the young Church was convinced that the Crucified One embraced every person, even the most wicked and desperate. Through the torn veil of Jesus' body, the boundaries between the sacred enclosure and the world without God are destroyed. Through Jesus everyone now has access to the Father.

Paul and the first Christian community always kept before their eyes this disturbing truth: the cross of Jesus is planted in the midst of a sinful world. Therefore, if we want to discover the Lord's face, we have to look for it among those who are furthest away. Jesus waits for us in every human being, whatever be his or her situation, his or her past, his or her state of life.

On the Mount of Olives before ascending to heaven, Jesus said to his disciples: "You will be my witnesses in Jerusalem and in all Judea and Samaria, all the way to the ends of the earth" (Acts 1:8). Like the Apostles, like Paul, we are called to go *extra muros,* to all people.

My most beautiful cathedral

During my voyage toward North Vietnam, I was put in chains three times with a man who was non-Catholic, a member of the parliament, and someone known for his fundamentalist Buddhism. Yet, being together in the same terrible situation touched his heart. Later I learned that after his liberation, he willingly related how he had felt honored to be chained with me and had, in fact, always tried to be chained with me, and that we had become friends.

On the ship and afterward in the re-education camp, I had occasion to dialogue with the most varied people: ministers, members of parliament, high civil and military figures, as well as religious authorities among the Cao Đài, Hoà Hảo, Buddhists, Brahmanists, Moslems, and people of different Protestant denominations including Baptists and Methodists. In the camp, I was elected bursar, which gave me the responsibility of serving everyone, distributing the food, getting the hot water, and carrying on my back the coal to keep us warm during the night. All this because the other prisoners considered me a man worthy of trust.

Upon my departure from Saigon, Jesus, crucified outside the walls of Jerusalem, made me understand that I had to engage in a new form of evangelization. I no longer acted as a bishop within a diocese, but *extra muros*; as a missionary *ad extra*, *ad vitam*, *ad summum*—going outside, for all my life, to the very limits of my capacity to love and give of myself. Now, yet another dimension opened itself, *ad omnes*—for all.

In the obscurity of faith, in service and in humiliation, the light of hope had changed my vision. I understood that at this point, on this ship, in this prison, was my most beautiful cathedral, and that these prisoners, without exception, were the people of God entrusted to my pastoral care. My prison was divine providence. It was the will of God.

I spoke of all of this to the other Catholic prisoners and there was born among us a profound communion, a new commitment. We were called to be together *witnesses of hope* for all people.

I cannot forget the great missionary adventure that developed in Vietnam. In the name of my people, I wish to express our special and profound gratitude to the universal Church, to the Congregation of the Propagation of the Faith, and to the courageous missionaries who brought the Gospel and shed their blood in our land as witnesses to the faith.

The radicality of the Gospel

In speaking of the adventure of hope, and in particular of evangelization, we are speaking of the radicality of the Gospel. I am struck by the fact that in Sacred Scripture, Jesus, Paul, and John often use words that express a dimension of absoluteness:

- That *all* may be one (cf. Jn 17:21), *all* people (cf. Mt 28:19).

- You shall love the Lord your God will *all* your heart, and with *all* your soul, and with *all* your mind (cf. Mt 22:37).

- Having loved his own who were in the world, he loved them *to the end* (cf. Jn 13:1).

- You will be my witnesses…to *the ends* of the earth (cf. Acts 1:8).

There are still other verses that express the infinite dimension of the work of evangelization:

- *As in heaven* so also on earth: the same love (cf. Jn 15:12), the same mission (cf. Jn 20:21).

- With each of the following *four dimensions* the love of Christ must be manifested in us: the length and breadth, the height and depth (cf. Eph 3:18–19).

I can understand why St. Maximilian Kolbe would habitually repeat: "Absolutely, totally, without condition." And Jesus summarizes everything on the cross: *consummatum est* ("it is finished") (Jn 19:30).

All things to all people

Only through the radicality of sacrifice can we be witnesses of hope inspired, as John Paul II writes, "by Christ's own charity, which takes the form of concern, tenderness, compassion, openness, availability, and interest in people's problems" (*Redemptoris Missio*, n. 89).

The figure of St. Paul accompanies us in this our mission:

> For though I am totally free, I have made myself a slave to all in order to win over as many as possible. I became a Jew for the Jews in order to win the Jews…. For those outside the Torah, I became like one outside the Torah…although I am under Christ's law. I have become all things to all people so that, by all means, I might win some of them over. I do all this for the sake of the good news… (1 Cor 9:19–23).

In his solidarity with the least, those furthest away, those without God, Jesus Crucified opened the apostolic way of "becoming all to all." Paul, in his turn, communicates to Christians their true apostolate: to reveal to every person, without discrimination, that God is close to them and loves them infinitely.

Making ourselves "one" with everyone, and having the courage to regard every human person—including those who seem most contemptible or hostile—as "neighbor," as brother or sister, we practice the central content of salvation. We live the joyful announcement that in the cross of Jesus, God comes close to every person who is far from God, to offer pardon and redemption. For this reason, evangelization is not a task that is entrusted to missionaries alone. It is an essential element in every Christian life. The Good News of God who is close can be manifested only if we make ourselves close to all people.

A limitless horizon: all for the Gospel

In concluding this meditation, let us allow the vast horizons of the Church's mission as outlined by the Second

Vatican Council—and witnessed to by the last few Popes—to again come before the eyes of our mind:

- *The whole person and each person* is the recipient of the Good News.

- The task of evangelization today urges us to undertake, concentrically, a *universal dialogue,* beginning within the Church, embracing the members of other churches and ecclesial communities, moving out toward the great religions, and establishing ties of friendship and cooperation also with those who do not profess a religious faith, and does not exclude even those who oppose and persecute the Church in different ways. "We are all called to be brothers," affirms *Gaudium et Spes* (n. 92).

- The almost 100 *pastoral trips* of John Paul II to the five continents speak eloquently of the illuminating ray of light we are called to cast in the service of the Gospel today. These journeys include his meeting with the Aborigines in Papua, New Guinea; his visit to the slave island in West Africa; his talks with Fidel Castro in Cuba; the recent dialogue with the Great Sheik of Al-Azhar in Cairo; and his work for peace among the peoples and religions of the Holy Land.

- The Holy See, in the last ten years, has enriched itself with *new dicasteries* and numerous departments in order to respond always better to this mission, and to harvest what Christ Crucified, in his boundless love, has sown everywhere. Through these, the Church not only gives but also receives.

It is a privilege for me to be able to participate in this great effort, having already lived and worked for many years in the Roman Curia. From this heart of the Church, I am a happy witness of the marvels the Holy Spirit works day after day to bring the Good News to the heart of every person, every culture, and every dimension of human life. I am grateful to be able to live in communion with all, bearing in my soul the words of Paul: *"I have made myself all things to all people, to save at least some of them."* And again: *"I do all this for the sake of the good news"* (1 Cor 9:23).

HOPE AGAINST ALL HOPE

10

My God, My God, Why Have You Abandoned Me?

Abandoned to the Father

> At my first hearing no one came to my aid—they all deserted me.... But the Lord came to my aid and strengthened me so that through me the proclamation of the good news might be fully accomplished (2 Tim 4:16–17).

These words of Paul reflect my own experience during the hard years of my imprisonment. Not that my faithful or my priests abandoned me, but no one was able to do anything for me. I remained completely isolated and I felt abandoned, but "the Lord stayed with me"; the Father, even when he is hidden, does not abandon us.

During the first months of my imprisonment, I found myself in the most Catholic part of the city of Nha Trang where I had been bishop for eight years.

From my cell, I could hear the bells of my cathedral ringing day and night, and throughout the whole day those of the parishes and religious communities nearby. I would have preferred to be in the mountains so that I would not have had to hear them.

In the silence of the night, I heard the sound of the ocean waves of the Pacific, which I used to watch from my office window. No one knew where to find me, though the prison was only a few kilometers away from my own house. Absurd life!

As I have already mentioned, on the evening of December 1, 1976, I was taken from the prison of Thủ Đức. I was to embark on the ship *Hải Phòng*. That evening as all the prisoners waited to set sail, we were told to sit down on the ground in the dark. At a distance of only 3 kilometers, I could see the lights of the city of Saigon, the center of the diocese of which I had been named coadjutor on April 24, 1975. I knew my journey would take me far away. The pain this caused me was agonizing. I thought of the Apostle Paul at Miletus, when he gathered the elders of Ephesus knowing that he would never see them again. And yet, I could not gather my own! I could not comfort them or give them any advice. Within myself, I said goodbye to all of them, and especially to my dear elderly Archbishop Phaolô Nguyễn Văn Bình, with a broken heart at the thought of never seeing him again. To this day, I have yet to see him again.

I experienced a profound pastoral suffering in all of this, but I can testify that the Father did not abandon me and that he gave me strength.

Our moments of abandonment

Perhaps all of us have lived similar moments of abandonment. At times we feel misunderstood, disappointed, betrayed. We notice the insufficiency of our strength and our solitude in the face of tasks that are bigger than we are. We encounter the atrocious sufferings of the Church, of whole peoples. The very light of faith and love seem to extinguish themselves at such moments and we fall into sadness and anguish.

There are small or smaller nights of the soul. Sometimes they are prolonged, and this darkens our certainty of the presence of God who is close and gives meaning to our lives.

There are nights that sometimes assume an epochal and collective dimension, as in our own times when the human person, as the Holy Father has so clearly observed, "notwith-standing his conquests, touches…the depths of abandonment, the temptation of nihilism, the absurdity of physical, moral, and spiritual suffering."[1]

Paul spoke of his more crucial moments of abandonment, "…in danger from my own people, danger from Gentiles, danger in the city, danger in the wilderness, danger at sea." At the end of this list he mentions what was for him the saddest fact, but one that brought him closer to Jesus: "Danger from false brothers and sisters" (cf. 2 Cor 11:26).

The mystery of the cross

It is the law of the Gospel that "…unless a grain of wheat falls to the earth and dies, it remains just a single grain; but if it dies, it bears much fruit" (Jn 12:24).

It is the law Jesus lived in the first person. His death was real, but even more real is the superabundant life springing from that death. But how much this life cost him!

He came down to earth for love of us, to accomplish, in full unity with the will of the Father, his design for the salvation of the world.

"Because of his infinite love for man," writes Maximus the Confessor, "he really and fully became in nature what he loved."[2]

Paul has us contemplate the ineffable *kenosis* of God in the famous hymn found in the Letter to the Philippians. Christ is presented in the act of stripping himself of his divine form in order to assume "the form of a slave" and become, in all things, similar to human beings (cf. 2:6–8).

---

1. *Teachings of John Paul II,* V/3. Città del Vaticano: 1982, pp. 1141–1142.

2. Maximus the Confessor, *Ambiuorum Liber:* PG 91, 1048.

This is the image of a God whose self-giving is without reserve. He gives his own life without measure, to the point of being lifted on a cross, where he takes upon himself all the sins of the world. He who is the "innocent one" (Mt 27:4–19, 24), the "just one" (1 Pet 3:18), assumes the appearance of sinful human beings.

"Christ redeemed us from the curse of the law (that is, from sin) by becoming a curse for us," Paul affirms in Galatians (cf. 3:13).

This was an admirable exchange between God and humanity which Augustine will call an "exchange of love," and Leo the Great, a "salutary exchange."[3]

The abandonment of Jesus

"God made him to be sin," we read in the Second Letter to the Corinthians (cf. 5:21).

There, on the cross, already close to death, Jesus turns to the Father crying: "My God, my God, why have you abandoned me?" (Mk 15:34; Mt 27:46).

This is the mysterious cry of a God who feels himself abandoned by God. At the summit of his life, Jesus has been betrayed, his own are no longer with him, and now God—that God whom he called Father, Abba—is silent. The Son feels the void of his absence, and loses the sense of his presence. The unshakable certainty of never being alone (cf. Jn 8:29), of always being heard by the father (cf. Jn 11:42), of being the instrument of his will (cf. Jn 8:29), gives way to a supplication full of anguish.

It seems that what was most his, his intimate union with the Father, has been obscured, and so much so that he no

---

3. St. Augustine, *Contra Faustum,* 5, 9: PL 42, 226; Leo the Great, *Sermo 54,* 4: PL 54, 321.

longer feels himself to be a son. He cries out, "My God, my God," and no longer, "Father."

John Paul II speaks of this mystery with touching depth:

> One can say that these words on abandonment are born at the level of that inseparable union of the Son with the Father, and are born because the Father "laid on him the iniquity of us all." They also foreshadow the words of St. Paul: "For our sake he made him to be sin who knew no sin." Together with this horrible weight, encompassing the "entire" evil of the turning away from God which is contained in sin, Christ, through the divine depth of his filial union with the Father, perceives in a humanly expressible way this suffering which is separation, the rejection by the Father, the estrangement from God.[4]

"That," says St. John of the Cross, "was the most desolate abandonment that he ever experienced in his senses during his life...in such a way that Christ remained annihilated, reduced almost to nothing."

"Yet," St. John of the Cross continues, "precisely in being oppressed, he accomplished more marvels than he had accomplished in heaven or on earth during his earthly existence rich in miracles and wonders, a work that consists in having reconciled and united humanity to God through grace."[5]

The summit of suffering reached by the Son of God is revealed as the summit of his love for us.

In her intense prayer, Chiara Lubich says:

> So that we would have light, you made yourself blind.
> So that we would be united, you experienced
> separation from the Father.

---

4. John Paul II, *Salvifici Doloris* (On the Christian Meaning of Human Suffering). Boston: Pauline Books & Media, 1984, n. 18.

5. St. John of the Cross, *The Ascent of Mount Carmel*, 1. 2, c. 7, par.11, in: *Opere*. Rome: 1979, p. 92.

So that we would possess wisdom, you became
    "ignorance."
So that we would be clothed again in innocence,
    you became "sin."
So that we would have hope, you almost despaired.
So that God would be in us, you experienced his
    distance.
So that heaven would be ours, you experienced hell.
To give us an easy journey on earth among hundreds of
    brothers, you expelled yourself from heaven and
    from earth, from men and from nature.
You are God. You are my God,
    our God of infinite love.[6]

One with the Father

Still, we know that in this extreme hour in which the Son felt himself abandoned by the Father, the Father also lives the same "passion of love" of the Son.[7]

In fact, in offering the Son—that is, in allowing the Son to cover the enormous distance from God provoked by sin—the Father, in a certain way, also enters into communion with all of suffering humanity. This is the point to which God's love for humanity brings him.

The Son, feeling himself abandoned by the Father, re-abandons himself to the Father with an act of infinite love: "Father, into your hands I commend my spirit" (Lk 23:46). Thus, he manifests himself to be one with the Father in love; one with him in that Spirit of love which binds them.

This experience of the most profound separation from God encloses within itself, in a mysterious and yet real way, the experience of the fullest union with the Father.

---

6. C. Lubich, *Perché Fosse Nostro il Cielo*, in: *Città Nuova*, 1975/3, p. 35.

7. Cf. Origen, *Homilia VI in Ezechielem*, 6: PG 13, 714.

As Pope John Paul II profoundly expressed:

> When the Son is abandoned by the Father in the Spirit, in that abandonment is contained the definitive fullness of that love which saves: the fullness of the unity of the Son with the Father in the Holy Spirit.[8]

In this astonishing and divine dynamic of love, each of our pains is gathered and transformed, every void filled, every sin redeemed. Our abandonment and our alienation from God are surmounted.

I fill up in my own flesh

There is a fathomless mystery in Jesus' cry of abandonment, in which he gathers every cry of humanity. This is a cry of labor for the "new creation," of our new birth as sons and daughters of God.

Yet, this labor is not accomplished without us. Jesus' extreme love impels us to live every suffering—as much as we are given—like him and in him.

And we can do it.

We can if, in each personal suffering and in those of others, we recognize a shadow of his infinite suffering, an aspect, an expression of his. Then, each time this suffering shows itself, we do not distance ourselves from it, but accept it fully as if we were accepting him. Forgetting ourselves, we cast our whole being into what God asks of us in the present moment, in the neighbor he places before us, motivated only by love. Then, very often we will see our sufferings vanish as if by some magic, and only love remains in the soul.

To treasure each suffering as one of the countless faces of Jesus crucified, and to unite our suffering to his, means to

---

8. *Teachings of John Paul II*, VIII/1. Città del Vaticano: 1986, p. 918.

enter into his own dynamic of suffering-love. It means to participate in his light, his strength, his peace; it means to rediscover within us a new and abundant presence of God.

I remember my own experience during my dark years of imprisonment. In the abyss of my sufferings, some feelings gave me peace of soul: I never ceased loving everyone, I never shut anyone out of my heart. "The God who is love is the one who will judge me," I told myself, "not the world, not the government, not propaganda. Everything passes, only God does not change. I am in the hands of Mary. I have to be faithful to the example of the martyrs who went before me, to the teaching I learned as a child from my mother."

For the sake of his body the Church

Uniting every suffering with Christ's on the cross means to become, with him and in him, instruments of salvation.

Here, I think of each of us as priests.

Why did the pilgrims to Ars, as one heart and one soul, press tightly around the altar where St. John Vianney celebrated the Eucharist? Why were those who participated at the Masses of Padre Pio so fascinated by the mystery he celebrated before them, to the point that they were no longer aware of the time that passed?

It is because they saw a priest so identified with Jesus on the cross that he could say, with St. Paul: "I am completing what is lacking in Christ's afflictions on behalf of his body, that is, the church" (Col 1:24).

Like the Curé of Ars and Padre Pio, in each of our Masses we have around us the entire world with all those places where "God cries," with all sinners and with all the sufferings of humanity. Let us hear with our ears, let us suffer in our hearts, and let us allow the Spirit to pray in us with "inexpressible groanings" (cf. Rom 8:26). Let us unite everything to Jesus crucified, who is there on the altar. Let us identify ourselves with him. Thus, in faith we can be "glad and shout for joy when his glory is revealed" (1 Pet 4:13).

Christ crucified is our hope.

"For just as Christ's sufferings overflow and include us, so too through Christ our encouragement is also unbounded" (2 Cor 1:5).

11
CAN THE BODY BE DIVIDED?
That the World May Believe

I still have before my eyes the ecumenical celebration of the opening of the Holy Door at the Basilica of St. Paul Outside the Walls, in the presence of eminent representatives of various churches and ecclesial communities.

I can still see the Holy Father kneeling on the threshold of the Holy Door, together with the Orthodox Metropolitan, Athanasius, and the Archbishop of Canterbury, George Carey. I see them lifting the book of the Holy Gospel toward the Four Corners of the earth and I see them exchanging the sign of peace.

I hear the cry of "Unity, unity," rising from the crowd of Catholics, Orthodox, and Protestants gathered at Bucharest in May of 1999, when John Paul II and Patriarch Teoctist offered each other the gift of a chalice.

A speedy journey toward a full and visible communion of Christians is a priority of the Jubilee Year 2000. We know how difficult and at the same time how urgent this communion is. We know that only a conversion of heart, only a special intervention of the Holy Spirit, can work this miracle.

For this reason, I would like to dedicate this meditation to ecumenism.

The cry of Jesus

When I see division among Christians, I think of the Body of Christ. "Can a body be divided? Can the Church, the Body of Christ, be divided?" were the questions that came vibrating—almost like a cry, an imploring cry—from the heart of the Holy Father at St. Paul Outside the Walls. In these questions, I feel St. Paul's dismay at the divisions within the community of Corinth when he asked: "Has Christ been divided?" (1 Cor 1:13)

I also hear in this the very cry of Jesus on the cross.

"Father, that they may be one...so that the world will believe" (cf. Jn 17:21) was his supreme prayer. Having come down to earth, he raised up the Church as "a people assembled in the unity of the Father, of the Son, and of the Holy Spirit" (cf. *Lumen Gentium*, n. 4). With the gift of the Eucharist, he made it his Body. With the sending of the Holy Spirit he forged it as the instrument to reunite all peoples in one family: "The Church is in Christ like a sacrament or as a sign and instrument both of a very closely knit union with God and of the unity of the whole human race" (*Lumen Gentium,* n. 1).

Yet, because of many sad events in history, and because of human weakness, those "baptized into one Spirit to form one body" (cf. 1 Cor 12:13) find themselves divided. Called to form the "instrument of unity," they are not united among themselves. This is the wound of the Church, the wound of Christ! How can the Good News make an impact? And with these presuppositions, how will we mend the rents of secularism and atheism that cause millions of people in lands of ancient Christian traditions to live as if God does not exist?

We are called, according to the perspective of Vatican Council II, to be prophets and leaven of unity in the bosom of humanity. How can we efficaciously accomplish this mission if already there are divisions among us? How can we carry out God's plan in history, overcoming the terrible economic disproportion that throws millions of human beings into an absolute poverty; the abolition of the logic of power and profit from which always new and devastating wars arise? How can we gather into one the diversity of peoples, cultures, and religions, if we Christians, if the Church of Christ, is not clearly a model of unity?

I hear in these questions the cry of Jesus: "My God, my God, why have you abandoned me?" and "I thirst." I thirst to see my Spirit, the Spirit of love, moving freely among you, among all the members of the Body. I thirst to see the baptized again become the instrument of unity. I thirst to see the fruit of my offering: Christians united in *one* Church!

"Unity, unity," cried the people of Bucharest. And at St. Paul Outside the Walls, John Paul II exclaimed: "Thank you for this voice, for this consoling voice of our brothers and of our sisters. Perhaps we can also leave this basilica crying like them, *'Unità, unità; unité; unity.'*"

Hope against all hope

A bishop who has experience in this area has said: "One enters into ecumenism with much hope, and one remains against all hope."

In 1994, John Paul II formulated the wish that "we can celebrate the Great Jubilee, if not completely united, at least much closer to overcoming the divisions of the second millennium" (*Tertio Millennio Adveniente*, n. 34). At the time, humanly speaking, the prospects for ecumenism were not the best. In those very years, new obstacles presented themselves on the journey toward a full and visible communion of Christians. A kind of pessimism grew. Nevertheless, unity is the work of the Holy Spirit.

It is said that during a particularly difficult moment, Max Thurian, who had worked for many years in the World Council of Christian Churches, was invited to resist discouragement. He responded, "Discouraged, never! One has to go ahead, everyone in his place, seriously and faithfully. Then, hopefully, when one least expects it, a passage will open through which history will make a quality step forward."

Some events, really right on the threshold of the Jubilee Year, give us hope for such a quality step.

The mutual Catholic-Lutheran declaration on the doctrine of justification was signed in Augsburg last October 31, 1999. Amid the exultation of the people and the emotion of those responsible for that event, many people present confided some similar sentiments. "It seemed to me that the Holy Spirit hovered over this Assembly and the weight of division would be alleviated; a happiness never before experienced!"

Concerning the Eastern Churches, significant steps have been made. After John Paul II's unforgettable visit to Romania, he was able to visit the sister-Orthodox Church in Georgia in November of 1999. Then, at the beginning of December, the Churches present in the Holy Land opened the Great Jubilee together at Bethlehem with a participation of people as never seen before.

A few days later, the study undertaken by the Church in the Czech Republic on the figure of Jan Hus[1] resulted in a meeting in the Pontifical Lateran University. This was an important stage of purification of memory, which has given further hope for the full reconciliation of Christians in that country.

Then came the historic encounter at the Basilica of St. Paul Outside the Walls, which witnessed the most numerous presence of representatives of different Churches from all over the world since Vatican Council II. The Metropolitan

---

1. Jan Hus, a Czech religious leader and reformer, was excommunicated in 1411 for his refusal to obey the Church's prohibition on preaching, and for failing to appear before the Roman Curia. In 1414, tried and convicted of heresy, he was burned at the stake.

Athanasius commented afterward: "Everyone has to repeat this action: accomplish conversion of heart."[2] And the Archbishop of Canterbury, George Carey, declared: "I was very encouraged to go forward."[3]

Full of amazement, we followed the Holy Father's visit to Egypt on February 24, 2000. What a witness to all Christians and to the world were the words of Patriarch Shenouda III, "We love you, your Holiness," and the response of the Holy Father, "I wish to exchange sentiments with you by saying: 'We love you, too!'"[4]

Finally, there has been the Holy Father's courageous confession of the blows against the unity of the Body of Christ. Made on the First Sunday of Lent of this Jubilee Year 2000, its impact continues to echo throughout the whole world!

The sacrifice of unity

In the cause of ecumenism "there is not a moment to lose," John Paul II reminds us with insistence. "At the beginning of a new century and of a new millennium, which leaves enormous challenges to the human family...this common witness is more important than ever."[5] Yet, according to human standards, the journey toward the full visible unity of all the baptized still seems very long.

I recall an episode related to me by Roger Schutz, the prior of Taizé. He was visiting Constantinople. "When we had already been dismissed," he told me, "the Patriarch Athenagoras unexpectedly came toward me again. With his hands lifted meaningfully as if holding a chalice, his eyes brilliant like a fire, and in a moving tone of voice, he said to me: 'This is unity!'"

---

2. Television Interview of SAT 2000 (Jan. 1, 2000).
3. Ibid.
4. *L'Osservatore Romano,* Feb. 27, 2000, p. 4–5.
5. Ibid.

I also remember the recent presence of Archbishop Carey here in Rome. "Every time I see the catacombs," he confided to me, "I feel near the Apostles. I feel I'm reliving the primitive Church." He also expressed his great regard for John Paul II and his longing for full communion.

Toward where can we look to achieve this highest and apparently so difficult goal?

The great challenge of the unity of the Church makes us root ourselves even more firmly in the unfathomable depths of the Paschal Mystery.

Jesus, who in the moment of his abandonment seemed to have lost his unity with the Father and with humanity, is *the image of the division* that exists among the churches. Discovering his face in this wound of divisions, and loving him passionately in this sad situation, we find the *strength not to avoid* the sufferings and difficulties that mark the way toward full communion. United to him on the cross, we find the strength to face them.

Passing with Jesus through the Holy Door of the cross, we can also find the *way to heal* the wounds of his body. It is really at the moment when he experienced the most profound separation that he gave birth to the Church. Placing ourselves there in the wound of division together with him, with immense love, we too can be instruments of unity. In his *kenosis* (emptying) for love, he teaches us the way to *énosis* (unity). In his radical descent and interior divestment of all riches, he shows us *the style and the measure* of the love that leads to unity.

In communion with him is the way:

- to overcome every self-sufficiency and to welcome one another;
- to re-open the doors that seem closed forever;
- to acknowledge our faults and to forgive one another;

- to love with that charity which "bears all things, believes all things, hopes all things, endures all things" (1 Cor 13:7).

On January 18, 2000, in the Basilica of St. Paul, Pope John Paul II referred to the conclusion of his encyclical, *Ut Unum Sint* (n. 102). He said: "The aspiration for unity moves forward at the same pace as a profound capacity for 'sacrifice.'" He went on to explain: "To predispose ourselves to sacrifice for unity means to change our outlook, to broaden our horizons, to know how to acknowledge the action of the Holy Spirit who works in our brothers, to discover new faces of holiness, to open ourselves to new aspects of the Christian commitment."[6]

Conversion of heart

Together with you, I would like to thank God for the great gift of unity, which comes to us from Christ crucified. Together with you, I would like to put myself again in Christ's footsteps, ready for that conversion of heart on which rests "true ecumenism."[7]

I was deeply touched by these words of the great Patriarch Athenagoras:

We need to succeed in disarming ourselves.
I have fought this war. For years and years.
It was terrible. But now I'm disarmed.
I am no longer afraid of anything,
because "love drives out fear."
I am disarmed of the will to overcome,
to justify myself at the expense of others.

---

6. *L'Osservatore Romano,* Jan. 19, 2000, p. 7.
7. Second Vatican Council, *Unitatis Redintegratio,* 1964, n. 7.

I am no longer on the alert,
jealously grasping my riches.
I welcome and I share.
I am not attached to my opinions, to my plans.
If other better proposals come to me,
I accept them willingly.
Or rather, not better, but good.
You know, I have given up comparisons….
That which is good, true, real, wherever it is,
it is the best for me.
Therefore, I am no longer afraid.
When you no longer possess anything,
you no longer have fear.
"Who can separate us from the love of Christ?"
But if we disarm ourselves,
if we divest ourselves,
if we open ourselves to the God-man
who makes all things new,
then it is he who cancels our evil past
and gives back to us a new time
where everything is possible.[8]

A new time: the time of unity. A time in which Christ crucified will see the full fruition of his self-offering. A time in which we will be able to say to those who think he is still entombed beneath the division of Christians: "He is not here. He is risen!" (cf. Mt 28:6)

8. Athenagoras, *Chiesa Ortodossa e Futuro Ecumenico. Dialoghi con Olivier Clément*. Brescia: 1995, pp. 209–211.

12

THE SEED OF CHRISTIANS
The Martyrs of Today

John Paul II has invited us, in this Great Jubilee, to open our eyes to the "new martyrs." A century like the one just completed, where there was a great sense of well-being, great attachment to life, and a great fear of losing it, was also a century of Christian martyrs. The martyrs lived among us. Indeed, they are the strength of the Church of the twentieth century and of the century just begun. We need to enlarge our perspective regarding this reality in the history of the Church in order to contemplate martyrdom.

The heritage of the martyrs

Within prison, I myself lived the suffering of the Church. I would notice time pass, day after day, without seeing its end. I would ask myself like the prophet Isaiah: "Sentinel, what remains of the night? Sentinel, what remains of the night?" (cf. Is 21:11) In those moments, I began to understand better the meaning of martyrdom, though not the bloody martyrdom which was, however, a possibility that loomed before me. I faced rather, the martyrdom of a life that places no limits on itself—out of the love of God, fidelity to the unity and communion of the Church, and the service of the Gospel—not even for the sake of self-preservation.

Christians certainly do not despise life. In prison, I would often recall the happy days of my pastoral service as a priest and a bishop. I would think of the Catholics in the dioceses where I had been, of my confreres, of my friends, and of my family. What joy it would have been to see them again!

And yet my faith could not be bargained with. It could not have been surrendered at any price, not even that of a happy life. I seemed to understand a little more that martyrdom does not place limits on loving the Lord, not even the very natural limit of saving oneself, one's own life, one's own happiness. At such times, I would think of the many Christians who were prisoners, suffering, deported. I would think of those who were undergoing great sufferings. I would remember the words from the Letter to the Hebrews: "In your struggle against sin you have not yet resisted to the point of shedding your blood…" (12:4).

I would find myself in communion with so many witnesses. "Therefore, since we are surrounded by so great a cloud of witnesses, let us put aside every burden and sinful entanglement and let us persevere and run the race that lies before us, let us keep our eyes fixed on Jesus, the pioneer and perfecter of faith" (Heb 12:1–2).

I would think of the persecutions, of the deaths, of the martyrdoms, that took place in the 350 years of Vietnam's history, which gave to the Church many unknown martyrs who number around 150,000.

I believe my priestly vocation is mysteriously but concretely linked to the blood of these martyrs—fallen in the last century while announcing the Gospel and remaining faithful to the unity of the Church, despite threats of death and violence.

I think of the witness of my paternal great-grandfather. He often told me of how the members of his family were forcibly separated and placed in the custody of different non-

Christian families in order to make them lose their faith, while his own father was imprisoned. So, at the age of 15, my great-grandfather would make a 30-kilometer journey on foot every day to bring his father the little rice and salt he had saved from what the family he lived with and worked for had given him. He would leave at 3:00 o'clock in the morning in order to return in time for work.

On the part of my maternal grandfather, there is one fact that is even more dramatic. In 1885, his entire parish community was burned alive in the church, with the exception of my grandfather who, at that time, was a student in Malaysia.

I believe that the fidelity of the Vietnamese Church can be explained with the blood of these martyrs. The priestly and religious vocations that enrich the Church in Vietnam are born from the grace of trials. The martyrs taught us to say *yes*—a yes without conditions and limits to the love of the Lord. But the martyrs also taught us to say *no*—no to flattery, to compromises, to injustice—even with the intent of saving one's own life and having a little tranquillity....

It is an inheritance, but one that has to be accepted. It is not automatic or the result of a natural course of events. It is possible to refuse it. The inheritance of the martyrs is not a matter of heroism but of fidelity. And fidelity is matured by turning one's gaze toward Jesus, who is the model of the Christian life, the model of every witness, and the model of every martyr.

Jesus: model and source of every martyrdom

In prison I wrote: "Look at the cross and you will find the solution to all the problems that assail you."[1] The martyrs looked to him....

---

1. F. X. Nguyễn Văn Thuận, *Five Loaves and Two Fish*, Cinisello Balsamo: 1997, p. 74.

All of us can see Jesus at his moment of martyrdom, alone, abandoned, crucified. The people thus proclaim the end of that Teacher from Galilee: "He saved others; let him save himself if this fellow is God's Messiah, the Chosen One!" (Lk 23:35). The many miracles, the healings, the resurrections, the teachings…. Why doesn't he save himself? The soldiers taunt him: "If you are the King of the Jews, save yourself!" (Lk 23:37). In the Gospel of Matthew, the scribes and the priests declare: "He saved others, but he cannot save himself! If he is the King of Israel, let him come down now from the cross, and we will believe in him. He trusted in God, let God deliver him now, if he wants him" (Mt 27:42–43).

Jesus does not save himself. "To save himself, Jesus could leave Jerusalem and hide somewhere else; in this way he could escape from the conspiracy that was about to be carried out. He could go away, taking the road that goes from Jerusalem to Jericho where, in the parable, he placed the encounter with the Good Samaritan…. Escaping Jerusalem, perhaps he would have been saved, but he does not do it. He did not do it…. He stays and offers his life, without seeking to save himself."[2]

The martyrs surely looked to Jesus; they did not heed the ironies or counsels of those who surrounded them: "Save yourself!" Jesus is the model for so many martyrs, he "who for the sake of the joy that lay before him…, endured the cross, and thought nothing of the shame of it, and is now seated at the right hand of God's throne" (Heb 12:2).

We do not know how many have looked to Jesus from the solitude of their prisons; in the final hours after being sentenced to death; in the long nights waiting for an assassin's hand which they know is imminent; in the cold of their cells; and in the pain and the fatigue of senseless marches. We do

---

2. A. Riccardi, *Le Parole della Croce*, Brescia: 1999, p. 13.

not know how many have raised their eyes toward Jesus crucified, and conformed their lives to his martyrdom. Many—many more than we believe. What was written in the Letter to the Hebrews has come to pass: "Think of Jesus, who endured so much hostility from sinners, and do not let your souls grow weary or lose your courage" (Heb 12:3).

Many thought of him and did not lose heart. They found a strength that confounded their executioners and those who considered them as vanquished—as fragile objects in their hands. Again, from the Letter to the Hebrews: "they found strength in their weakness" (cf. 11:34). We can imagine the amazement of executioners at the sight of such strength from bodies already conquered and from an imprisoned existence!

An immense multitude
in the Church of today

These are not old stories out of the past! These are not only the stories of St. Ignatius of Antioch, who said: "It is beautiful to fade from the world for the Lord, and to rise again with him." We must know how to discern the visions of the Book of Revelation in the history of the twentieth century:

> After this I looked, and behold a vast crowd which no one could ever count from every nation, tribe, people, and tongue, standing before the throne and the Lamb and dressed in long white robes with palm branches in their hands. They were crying out in a loud voice and saying, "Salvation belongs to our God who is seated on the throne, and to the Lamb!" (Rev 7:9–11)

Who are "they"? The ancient one says: "These are they who came through the terrible persecution. They washed their robes and made them white in the blood of the Lamb" (7:14). They are those who have not renounced love to save their own life. They are those who have believed that salvation belongs to our God.

Opening our eyes and reading this vision in our times, we will see a great crowd of martyrs, the new martyrs of the twentieth century. We are not dealing only with a few examples. They are not rare exceptions, but an immense multitude that is difficult to count—hundreds of thousands of men and women. Many testimonies about them have not reached us. Others have been jealously guarded in the records of executioners. The names of others have been tarnished, adding disgrace to martyrdom. They are "an immense multitude that no one can count."

They belong to diverse nations, speak different languages, and have different features. Many people, many churches, many communities have suffered. John Paul II says in *Tertio Millennio Adveniente*:

> At the end of the second millennium, the Church has once again become a Church of martyrs. The persecutions of believers—priests, religious, and laity—has caused a great sowing of martyrdom in different parts of the world. The witness to Christ borne even to the shedding of blood has become a common inheritance of Catholics, Orthodox, Anglicans, and Protestants…" (n. 37).

Meditating on the martyrology of the twentieth century, some words of Sacred Scripture appear to me as the columns supporting this glorious monument:

"For apart from me you can do nothing" (Jn 15:5).

"I can do everything through the One who strengthens me" (Phil 4:13).

"It was not I, it was the grace of God working in me" (1 Cor 15:10).

Martyrs of charity

I would like to remember for a moment the "kingdom of the wretched," as one deportee called it, the prison camp in the Solovetsky Islands of Russia.

One detainee remembered an image of love in the midst of that hell:

> Uniting their efforts, a Catholic bishop who was still young worked together with an emaciated old man—an Orthodox bishop with a white beard, ancient in days but strong in spirit, who energetically pushed the load.... Any of us who would one day have the good fortune of returning to the world, would have to testify to what we had seen here and now. What we saw was the rebirth of the pure and authentic faith of the early Christians: the union of Churches in the persons of the Catholic and Orthodox bishops who participated unanimously in the duties, united in love and humility.[3]

This happened in Solovetsky, "alma mater" of the Soviet prison camps. John Paul II said: "Perhaps the most convincing form of ecumenism is the ecumenism of the saints and of the martyrs. The holy *communio sanctorum* (communion of saints) speaks louder than the things which divide us."[4]

Among the *martyrs of Soviet Communism*, we can remember only a few faces. Many of the names are known only to God. The Orthodox Metropolitan Benjamin of Petersburg, martyred in 1922 after a trial based on false accusations, wrote this before his execution:

> Times have changed and now we have the possibility of suffering for the love of Christ—sufferings both from

---

3. J. Brodskij, Solovki: *Le Isole del Martirio.* Milan: 1998, p. 152.
4. John Paul II, *Tertio Millennio Adveniente* (On Preparation for the Jubilee of the Year 2000). Boston: Pauline Books & Media, 1994, n. 37.

our own people and from foreigners. Suffering is hard and heavy, but according to the measure of our suffering, divine consolations superabound. It is difficult to cross…this boundary and to entrust oneself totally to the will of God. But when this happens, man is filled with consolation, he no longer feels these terrible sufferings….[5]

These terrible sufferings did not weaken the many witnesses in the *Nazi camps*. Even there, love was lived, as demonstrated by the life of St. Maximilian Kolbe, patron of the difficult twentieth century. He did not consider his own survival to be the supreme value of his life—"strong as death is love" (Song 8:6). The inhumanity of the concentration camps—that terrible underworld, school of hate and annihilation of the person—did not suffocate that love which is strong to the point of martyrdom. "Many waters cannot quench love," continues the Song of Songs, "neither can floods drown it" (8:7).

A multitude of martyrs spoke languages different from those people among whom they died—the *missionaries* who did not leave their communities at the moment of danger and who died while other foreigners escaped. Missionary martyrs whose fear did not extinguish love. Martyrs of love. In 1995, six members of the Sisters of the Poor of Bergamo died in the Ebola epidemic in the Congo. Despite the danger of infection, the sisters that stayed chose to remain behind in order to take care of the sick. Others arrived to help them. They all died. One of them, Sr. Dinarosa, was asked: "Aren't you afraid, being always in the midst of the sick?" She responded: "My mission is to serve the poor. What did my Founder do? I am here to follow in his footsteps…the Eternal Father will help

5. O. Vasil'eva, *Russia Martire: La Chiesa Ortodossa dal 1917–1941*. Milan: 1999, p. 95.

me." They were martyrs of love. For the Christian, protecting one's own life is not the absolute value. Love for the poor counts more than saving self.

Martyrs for the faith. The Armenian Catholic bishop of Mardin, Monsignor Maloyan, a man of peace, was unjustly accused, arrested, and forced to march at length with a contingent of Christians. Some proposed that he renounce his faith in order to save himself. He responded: "We will die, but we will die for Jesus." He died a martyr with his faithful in 1915.

Martyrs of ethnic hatred. At the seminary of Buta in a Burundi tormented by ethnic wars, forty Hutu and Tutsi seminarians were massacred together on April 30, 1996, by Hutu guerrillas. They had been told to divide themselves into two groups—Hutus and Tutsi. By doing so, the Hutus would have saved their lives, but they refused to separate themselves from their companions and all were killed.

We cannot describe the wonders of grace in so many of our brothers and sisters whose suffering is known only to God. Brothers and sisters, we will not forget you!

Witnesses of the Passover of Christ

How many martyrs! A crowd of martyrs: martyrs for purity, martyrs for justice, child martyrs, men and women martyrs, and martyred peoples. This great fresco stretches out before our eyes—one of a Christian humanity, meek, humble, non-violent, resisting evil, weak and at the same time strong in the faith—people who have loved and believed beyond death. This martyred humanity is the hope of the century we are beginning to live.

This is a heritage for the Christians of the twenty-first century, one that we must embrace and choose. It is a heritage to embrace in everyday life, in the small and great difficulties, in the stripping away of all aggressiveness, of all hatred, of all violence. The heritage of the martyrs is accepted every day in a life full of love, meekness, and fidelity. Isaac the Syrian wrote: "Let yourself be persecuted, but you, do not persecute. Let yourself be crucified, but you, do not crucify. Let yourself be abused, but you, do not abuse."[6]

I seem to hear a question being asked of all of us in this Lent and Easter of the Great Jubilee. Do we desire to embrace the heritage of these martyrs beneath the sign of the Cross and of the Resurrection?

"I saw my father go up to Heaven"

A small book by this title won the UNESCO prize. In it the author, a Russian who lives in Paris, describes the life of his father with moving words. His father was an Orthodox priest, a pious and passionate pastor who made countless sacrifices in the midst of persecution. One day during the war he was arrested because he was wearing a pair of shoes that one of his sons, a soldier, had given him. He was condemned to death because the law forbade civilians to wear military shoes. This was of course merely a pretext to conceal the real motive for his condemnation: his religious activity.

The whole village was convened around the pastor on an open field. The captain declared the sentence, and the priest's entire response was to kneel down and pray. All the people knelt with him and prayed aloud. "Fire," commanded the captain. But the soldiers stood there motionless. "Fire!" he cried again. No one fired. Finally, defeated, the captain could do nothing other than to allow the priest to return on horseback to his home with his people.

---

6. *Discorsi Ascetici*, 58, cited from O. Clément, *Alle Fonti con I Padri: I Mistici Cristiani delle Origini. Testi e Commento*. Rome: 1987, p. 270.

Some months later, while on a pastoral journey, this Orthodox priest "vanished." No one ever heard any more about him, but everyone understood his fate. His people said that he had gone to heaven on his horse.

O Crux, ave spes unica,
mundi salus et gloria!

Hail, O Cross, our one hope,
salvation and glory of the world!

13

In Prayer to God

To Pray Always

After my liberation from prison many people said: "Father, you must have had a lot of time to pray in prison." It is not as simple as one would think. The Lord allowed me to experience all my weakness, my physical and mental fragility.

Time passes slowly in prison, above all in isolation. Imagine a week, one month, two months and more...of silence. They are terribly long, but when they become years, they are an eternity. There were days when, exhausted by fatigue and sickness, I did not manage to say a single prayer!

It is true that one can learn much about prayer, about the genuine spirit of prayer, precisely when one suffers at not being able to pray because of physical weakness, the inability to concentrate, and spiritual aridity. We learn much from the feeling of being abandoned by God and being so far from him that we cannot say a word to him.

Perhaps it is at just such moments that we discover the essence of prayer and understand how to live the command of Jesus: "You must pray always" (cf. Lk 18:1).

From the Desert Fathers to the Russian Pilgrims, from the monks of the West to those of the East, there has been one fundamental preoccupation, one passionate search: that of being able to practice a persevering and continual prayer. "This is the culmination of perfection," says St. John Cassian.

"That all of our life, every movement of our heart, becomes a unifying and uninterrupted prayer."[1]

A simple prayer

I love to pray with the prayers of the liturgy, the psalms, and the canticles. I really love Gregorian chant, which I know mostly by heart. Thanks to my seminary formation, these liturgical songs profoundly entered my heart! Then, there are the prayers in my native language, which my whole family recited every evening in our home chapel, so moving, and which recall my earliest childhood—above all, the three *Hail Mary's* and the *Memorare* that my mother taught me to recite morning and evening.

I love the prayer of St. Francis of Assisi who spent an entire night in the snow, repeating: "My God and my All!" Also the prayer of Don Marmion, abbot of Maredsous: "My God, my Mercy!" Among the ways to live the spirit of prayer, there are, in fact, those brief arrows to heaven, those short prayers that nothing on earth can impede because they are the breath of the soul, the beating of the heart.

I look to Jesus as a model of prayer. His prayer, sincere and simple, is directed toward the Father. His prayer might be long and without formulas, like the ardent and spontaneous priestly prayer after the Last Supper.

Often, however, Jesus, the Virgin Mary, and the Apostles, used short but very beautiful prayers that they associated to their daily life. I, who am weak and tepid, love these brief prayers before the tabernacle, at the desk, on the street, when alone. The more I repeat them the more I am penetrated by them:

---

1. St. John Cassian, *Conferenze*, 10, 7: SC 54, 81.

"Here I am, the servant of the Lord" (Lk 1:38).

"My soul magnifies the Lord" (Lk 1:46).

"They have no more wine" (Jn 2:3).

"Father, forgive them, for they do not know what they do" (Lk 23:34).

"Behold your son.... Behold your mother" (cf. Jn 19:26–27).

"Jesus, remember me when you come into your kingdom" (Lk 23:42).

"Father, into your hands I commend my spirit" (Lk 23:46).

"What am I to do, Lord?" (Acts 22:10)

"Lord, you know everything, you know that I love you" (Jn 21:17).

"God, be merciful to me, a sinner" (Lk 18:13).

All of these short prayers, one connected to the other, form a life of prayer. Like a chain of discreet gestures, of glances, of intimate words, they form a life of love. They keep us in an atmosphere of prayer without taking us away from our present duty, and they help us to sanctify everything.

In the state of prayer

What can help us in our everyday life, in the normal routine of work and relationships, to maintain a state of prayer, of union with God?

Reading the Desert Fathers—for whom solitude was a *conditio sine qua non* ("condition without which, not") of continuous prayer—I was impressed by a very meaningful episode. It is said that one day the great Anthony had a surprising revelation: "In the city there is someone who resembles you. He belongs to the medical profession, gives his surplus to the needy, and all day long sings the 'Holy, holy, holy' with the angels."[2]

How did this unknown doctor of Thebaid manage to practice so high a form of prayer? Perhaps Augustine gives the key when he affirms: "Your *desire* is your *prayer*; if your desire is constant, your prayer is constant."[3]

For Augustine, that *desire* is identified with *charity,* and *charity* leads us to do good. Thus, another way of rendering prayer continual is by doing good.

> Who is able to repeat the praises of God all day long? Who can persevere in praising God all day? I suggest to you a means with which you can praise God all day, if you want. All that you do, do well, and you have given praise to God.[4]

To be prayer

The last stage of continuous prayer, according to spiritual authors, is when we not only pray always, but when we become prayer. Isaac of Niniveh describes the one who lives this way:

> Whether one eats, drinks, sleeps or whatever other thing one does, and even in the most profound sleep, the perfume of prayer rises without fatigue from one's heart.... The purified movements of the heart and of the intellect are voices full of sweetness with which such men never cease to sing in secret to the hidden God.[5]

---

2. *Vita e Detti dei Padri de Deserto.* Rome: 1999, p. 88.

3. *Enarrationes in Psalmos,* 37, 14: PL 36, 404.

4. Ibid., 34, II, 16: PL 36, 341.

5. Isaac of Niniveh, *Discorsi Ascetici,* 85, cited from O. Clément, *Alle Fonti con I Padri.* Rome: 1987, p. 205.

A modern expert in spirituality has condensed into a few words the whole tradition and contemporary feeling about prayer, saying:

> The true journey of prayer is life…. A continuous prayer is a life completely given to the service of God. This is the only manner of praying always. Prayer is continuous when love is continuous. Love is continuous when it is only one and complete.[6]

If our life becomes "a unique act of love extended through time," if it reflects in each moment the life of the Lord Jesus, then it is possible to understand this simple and concise thought from Chiara Lubich: "How does one manage to pray always? By being Jesus. Jesus prays always."

In this brief formula is contained the whole essence of prayer, in which it is Jesus himself who, as St. Augustine says, "*orat pro nobis ut sacerdos noster; orat in nobis ut caput nostrum; oratur a nobis ut Deus noster*" ("prays for us as our priest, prays in us as our head, is prayed to by us as our God").[7]

When one is unable to pray

There have been long periods in my life when I have suffered because of being unable to pray. I experienced the depth of my physical and mental weakness. Many times, I cried like Jesus on the cross: "My God, why have you abandoned me?" Yet, I know God did not abandon me.

Some of the police at the prison had studied Latin in order to be able to read the Church documents. One day one of them asked me:

"Can you teach me a Latin song?"

---

6. E. Ancilli, *Il Mistero della Preghiera Cristiana* in: *La Preghiera. Bibbia. Teologia. Esperienze Storiche.* Rome: 1988, p. 34.

7. *Enarrationes in Psalmos, 85,* 1: PL 37, 1081.

"Yes, but there are many of them, one more beautiful than the other."

"You sing and I will listen and pick one."

So I sang: *Ave Maris Stella, Salve Mater, Veni Creator...* and he chose the *Veni Creator!*

I would never have believed that an atheistic policeman would learn this entire hymn by heart, much less that he would start to sing it every morning at 7:00 A.M. when he came down the prison's wooden steps to go outside for his exercise and bath in the garden. He sang the hymn several times to accompany his various actions: "*Veni Creator Spiritus, mentes tuorum visita....*" Then he finished it while dressing in his room: "*in saeculorum saecula. Amen.*"

At first, I was surprised. Then little by little I realized that the Holy Spirit was using a communist policeman to help an imprisoned bishop pray when he was too weak and depressed to be able to pray. Only a policeman could have sung the *Veni Creator* in a loud voice. I would never have been permitted to, because it would have revealed to others that a priest was in that cell.

When it is impossible to pray, I turn to the Blessed Virgin, saying: "Mother, you see that I'm at the extreme limits. I cannot manage to recite any prayer. So then, I will say only 'Hail Mary,' with all my affection. Putting everything in your hands I will repeat: 'Hail Mary.' I ask you to distribute this prayer to all those in need, in the Church, in my diocese...." To put me in a state of prayer, it helps me to try to be a living Hail Mary

Another way that has helped me to pray has to do with is the Lord's Prayer. When, weakened and without strength, I could not even manage to pray this prayer, I thought of the Our Father in a brief and very concise formula:

For the Father: *your* name, *your* reign, *your* will.

For humanity: *our* bread, *our* debts, *our* temptations.

It is impossible to imagine the strength infused into the soul by the prayers of the liturgy. In prison when I felt depressed, I sang the hymn of the vespers for the martyrs *(Sanctorum Meritis)*, and every time it was like a powerful injection of the Holy Spirit that renewed my strength:

> *Ceduntur gladiis more bidentium*
> *non murmur resonat non querimonia;*
> *sed corde impavido mens bene conscia*
> *conservat patientiam.*[8]

They are given over to the sword
as sheep for the slaughter;
no murmur is heard, nor complaint,
but with fearless heart and fully aware
they bear all sufferings patiently.

The Testament of Jesus

The last example of my prayer as a bishop in prison is how I immersed myself in the *Testament of Jesus*: in his final words, in his final actions.

"What did Jesus leave us before going to heaven?" I would ask myself.

The answer: "He left us his Word, his Body, his Mother, his Church, his priesthood and his peace."

In his infinite love, *in finem dilexit* ("he loved them to the end"), he left us everything.

Then a wave of happiness would engulf me.

"What did Jesus promise us?" I would then ask myself. I would remember how much he promised his own before

---

8. *Liber Usualis,* p. 1158.

going back to the Father: that he would be with us every day until the end of the world (cf. Mt 28:20); that he would send us the Holy Spirit (cf. Jn 14:16–26); that the Father loves us (cf. Jn 16:27); that we can obtain everything we ask for in his name (cf. Jn 14:13); that wherever two or three of us gathered in his name, he would be in our midst (cf. Mt 18:20).

"What does Jesus ask of his Church?" I would ask further.

I would note that Jesus wanted to leave a poor Church—he who did not have a house in which to eat the Last Supper, and who offered the supreme sacrifice on the cross, stripped of his clothes.

Jesus wanted to leave a Church of service—he who washed the feet of his Apostles.

Jesus wanted to leave a Marian Church—he who from the height of the cross entrusted Mary to John and sent his Spirit upon them.

Jesus wanted to leave a missionary Church—he who sent the Apostles as his witnesses to the ends of the earth.

Jesus wanted to leave a Church that courageously faces the challenges of the world. He prayed: "I do not pray for you to take them out of the world, but for you to preserve them from the evil one" (cf. Jn 17:15).

And finally, I would ask myself: "What is the greatest commandment that he left us?" The answer was: "Love to the point of unity."

The *Testament of Jesus* is the inexhaustible treasure that nourished my spiritual life, preserving my hope in the trials of despair, solitude, sickness, on the sea, in the mountains, and in captivity.

Watch and pray

Permit me, brothers, to conclude this meditation with a prayer:

It is through prayer that I live in you, Lord.
My soul is in you, as a baby is in the womb of his mother,
his breath united to hers,
a heart that beats to the rhythm of the other's....

Lord Jesus, you are my model.
The Gospel shows you in prayer
for an entire night on the mountain.
You prayed before you worked a miracle,
before you chose your Apostles,
during the Last Supper....
You prayed while from your brow
flowed sweat and blood
in the garden of Gethsemane,
and while you agonized on the cross.

You prayed with the Word of God....
Your existence was a continuous prayer.

Turned toward the Father with a loving heart,
you were all at the service of his glory:
"May your name be holy,
your kingdom come."

You waited with ardor
for the coming of your hour
to accomplish the sacrifice of love.

You said:
"The Father and I are one."
"Pray without ceasing."
"I do always what is pleasing to my Father."

Thus, you make me understand
that incessant prayer
is communion with the Father,
and in practice this always consists
in doing the will of the Father
under the action of the Holy Spirit.

THE PEOPLE OF HOPE

14

MY FLESH FOR THE LIFE OF THE WORLD
One Body and One Blood in Christ

"The year 2000," we read in *Tertio Millennio Adveniente,* "will be intensely Eucharistic: in the Sacrament of the Eucharist the Savior, who took flesh in Mary's womb twenty centuries ago, continues to offer himself to humanity as the source of divine life."[1] And we are preparing ourselves to make Rome the *statio Orbis* ("residence of the world") with the celebration of the International Eucharistic Congress.

The food of witnesses

In 1975, when I was imprisoned, a tormenting question dominated my thoughts, "Will I be able to celebrate the Eucharist?" Later, the faithful asked me the same question. As soon as they saw me, they asked, "Were you able to celebrate the Holy Mass?"

When everything was lacking, the Eucharist, the Bread of Life, was uppermost in our thoughts. "If anyone eats of this bread he will live forever, and the bread that I will give for the life of the world is my flesh" (Jn 6:51).

---

1. John Paul II, *Tertio Millennio Adveniente* (On Preparation for the Jubilee of the Year 2000). Boston: Pauline Books & Media, 1994, n. 55.

How many times I recalled the expression of the fourth-century martyrs of Abitina who said, "We cannot live without the Lord's supper."[2]

At all times, and especially in times of persecution, the Eucharist has been the secret of the Christian life, the food of witnesses, and the bread of hope.

Eusebius of Cesarea tells us that the Christians did not neglect to celebrate the Eucharist, even in the midst of persecutions: "Every place where we suffered became for us a place to celebrate…whether it was a field, a desert, a ship, an inn, a prison…."[3] The martyrology of the twentieth century is filled with poignant accounts of clandestine celebrations of the Eucharist in concentration camps, because without the Eucharist we cannot live God's life!

"In memory of me"

At the Last Supper, Jesus lives the culmination of his earthly ordeal—the greatest self-giving in love toward the Father and toward humanity expressed in his sacrifice, which he anticipated in his body given and blood outpoured.

From this culminating moment—and from no other, however luminous and sparkling it may be, like the transfiguration or one of his miracles—Jesus leaves us the memorial. He leaves in the Church the memorial-presence of that supreme moment of love and of suffering on the cross, which the Father renders everlasting and glorious with the resurrection. To live of him, to live and die as he did.

Jesus desires that the Church remembers and lives the sentiments and the consequences of this memorial through

---

2. Cf. John Paul II, *Dies Domini* (On Keeping the Lord's Day Holy). Boston: Pauline Books & Media, 1998, n. 46.

3. Eusebius of Cesarea, *Historia Ecclesiastica* VII, 22, 4: PG 20, 687–688.

his living presence. "Do this in remembrance of me" (cf. 1 Cor 11:24).

Once more, I return to my own experience. When I was arrested, I had to leave immediately with empty hands. The next day, I was permitted to write to my people in order to ask for the most necessary things: clothes, toothpaste.... I wrote, "Please send me a little wine as medicine for my stomachache." The faithful understood right away.

They sent me a small bottle of wine for Mass with a label that read, "medicine for stomachaches." They also sent some hosts, which they hid in a flashlight for protection against the humidity.

The police asked me, "You have stomachaches?"

"Yes."

"Here's some medicine for you."

I will never be able to express my great joy! Every day, with three drops of wine and a drop of water in the palm of my hand, I would celebrate Mass. This was my altar, and this was my cathedral! It was true medicine for soul and body, "Medicine of immortality, remedy so as not to die but to have life always in Jesus,"[4] as St. Ignatius of Antioch says.

Each time I celebrated the Mass, I had the opportunity to extend my hands and nail myself to the cross with Jesus, to drink with him the bitter chalice. Each day in reciting the words of consecration, I confirmed with all my heart and soul a new pact, an eternal pact between Jesus and me through his blood mixed with mine. Those were the most beautiful Masses of my life!

Anyone who eats of me will live for me

So, for many years I was nourished with the bread of life and the chalice of salvation.

---

4. *Ad Eph.* 20, 2: *Patres Apostolici*, I, Ed. F. X. Funk, pp. 230–231.

We know that the sacramental aspect of the food that nourishes and the drink that fortifies suggests the life that Christ gives us and the transformation he accomplishes. "The true effect of the Eucharist is the transformation of man in Christ,"[5] affirm the Fathers. Leo the Great says: "The participation in the body and blood of Christ does nothing other than change us into what we receive."[6] Augustine gives voice to Jesus with this phrase: "You will not change me into yourself, as you do with bodily food, but you will be transformed into me."[7] Through the Eucharist we become, as Cyril of Jerusalem says: "one flesh and one blood with Christ."[8] Jesus lives in us and we in him in a kind of "symbiosis" and mutual indwelling. He lives in me, remains in me, acts through me.

The Eucharist in the re-education camp

Thus, in prison, I felt beating within my heart the same heart of Christ. I felt that my life was his life and his was mine.

The Eucharist became for me and for the other Christians a hidden and encouraging presence in the midst of all our difficulties. Jesus was adored secretly by the Christians who lived with me, just as happened so often in other prison camps of the twentieth century.

In the re-education camp, we were divided into groups of fifty people; we slept on a common bed, and everyone had a right to 50 centimeters of space. We managed to make sure that there were five Catholics with me. At 9:30 P.M. we had to

---

5. Cf. St. Thomas Aquinas, *In IV Sent.*, d. 12, q. 2, a. 1: *Opera Omnia*, X. Paris: 1839, p. 307.

6. Cf. *Serm.* 63, 7: PL 54, 357, taken from *Lumen Gentium* (Dogmatic Constitution on the Church), n. 25.

7. *Conf.*, VII, 10, 16: PL 32, 742.

8. *Cat.* Myst. 4, 3: PG 33, 1100.

turn off the lights and everyone had to go to sleep. It was then that I would bow over the bed to celebrate the Mass by heart, and I distributed communion by passing my hand under the mosquito net. We even made little sacks from the paper of cigarette packs to preserve the Most Holy Sacrament and bring it to others. The Eucharistic Jesus was always with me in my shirt pocket.

Every week there was an indoctrination session in which the whole camp had to participate. My Catholic companions and I took advantage of the breaks in order to pass the small sack to everyone in the four other groups of prisoners. Everyone knew that Jesus was in their midst. At night, the prisoners would take turns for adoration. With his silent presence, the Eucharistic Jesus helped us in unimaginable ways. Many Christians returned to a fervent faith-life, and their witness of service and love had an ever greater impact on the other prisoners. Even Buddhists and other non-Christians came to the faith. The strength of Jesus' love was irresistible.

In this way, the darkness of the prison became a paschal light, and the seed germinated in the ground during the storm. The prison was transformed into a school of catechesis. Catholics baptized fellow prisoners and became the godparents of their companions.

In Vietnam during this period, approximately 300 priests were imprisoned. Their presence within the different camps was providential, but not only for the Catholics. It became the occasion for a prolonged interreligious dialogue, which created an understanding and friendship with everyone.

Thus, Jesus became, as St. Teresa of Avila says, our true "companion in the Most Holy Sacrament."[9]

---

9. St. Teresa of Avila, *Libro de la Vida,* cap. 22, n. 6.

One bread, one body

Jesus made us to be Church.

"Because there is one bread, we who are many are one body" (1 Cor 10:17). Here is the Eucharist that makes the Church, the Eucharistic body that makes us the Body of Christ. To use a Johannine image, all of us are one vine, with the divine sap of the Spirit flowing through each and all (cf. Jn 15).

Yes, the Eucharist makes us one in Christ. Cyril of Alexandria wrote: "To establish us in unity with God and among ourselves, to join us to one another, the only-begotten Son… contrived a marvelous way: by means of one body, his own body, he sanctifies the faithful in the mystical communion, making them one body with himself and among themselves."[10]

We are one reality—that "one" which we become in the participation of the Eucharist. The Risen Christ makes us "one" with him and with the Father in the Spirit. In the unity realized by the Eucharist and lived in reciprocal love, Christ can take in hand the destiny of humanity and bring it to its true end: only one Father and all brothers and sisters.

Our Father, our bread

If we are aware of what the Eucharist accomplishes, that will immediately cause us to connect two phrases from the Lord's Prayer: "Our Father" and "our bread." The beginning of the Church testifies to this connection: "They devoted themselves…to the breaking of bread," says the Acts of the Apostles (2:24). Then it indicates the immediate reflection in the life of the community: "Now the whole group of those who believed were of one heart and soul, and no one claimed

10. *In Ioan. Ev.*, 11, 11: PG 74, 560.

private ownership of any possessions, but everything they owned was held in common" (Acts 4:32).

If the Eucharist and communion are two inseparable facets of the same reality, this communion cannot be only spiritual. We are called to give to the world a demonstration of a community where not only the faith is lived in common, but joys and sorrows as well; and where spiritual and material goods and needs are truly shared.

The ministry that I carry out in the heart of the Roman Curia at the service of justice and of peace renders me particularly sensitive to this obligation. It urges me to testify that the body of Christ is really "flesh for the life of the world."

We all know how, in the last two centuries, many who felt the need for true social justice, not finding a clear, strong witness within Christian environments, turned to false hopes. We have all been witnesses of true tragedies, some only heard of in reports, and some paid for with personal sacrifice.

In our day, social problems have not at all diminished. Sad to say, a great part of the world's population continues to live in the most inhuman misery. Now there is a trend toward globalization in all areas, which runs the risk of aggravating problems rather than resolving them. An authentic unifying principle is lacking, one that unites, values, and does not standardize the human person. What is missing is the principle of communion and of universal brotherhood: Christ, the Eucharistic bread that makes us one in him and teaches us to live according to that Eucharistic style of communion.

Christians are called to give this essential contribution. The Christians of the first centuries understood this very well. We read in the *Didaché*: "If we share heavenly goods, why not also share material goods?"[11] St. John Chrysostom exhorts us to be attentive to the presence of Christ in our brothers

_____

11. *Patres Apostolici,* IV, 8: I, Ed. F. X. Funk, pp. 12–13.

and sisters when we celebrate the Eucharist: "He who said: 'This is my body'…and who guaranteed with his word the truth of things, has also said this: what you refused to do for the least of these, you have refused to do for me."[12] Mindful of this, Augustine had a *domus caritatis* ("house of charity") constructed at Hippo near his cathedral. St. Basil gave life to a citadel of charity at Cesarea. The *Catechism of the Catholic Church* states that: "The Eucharist commits us to the poor. To receive in truth the Body and Blood of Christ given up for us, we must recognize Christ in the poorest, his brethren (cf. Mt 25:40)."[13]

However, the social function of the Eucharist extends further. The Church that celebrates the Eucharist is also to be capable of changing the unjust structures of this world into new social forms, into economic systems where the sense of communion rather than of profit prevails.

Paul VI created this stupendous program: "To make the Mass a school of profound spirituality and a peaceful but demanding training ground for Christian sociology."[14]

Jesus, the Bread of Life, urges us to work so that there will be no lack of that bread which so many still need:

- The *bread of justice* and of peace where war threatens, and where respect for the rights of persons, of families, of peoples, does not exist;

- The *bread of true freedom,* where a just religious freedom to profess one's own faith openly is not in force;

- The *bread of brotherhood*, where a sense of universal communion in peace and goodwill is not acknowledged or realized;

---

12. *In Mt. Hom.*, 5O, 3, 4: PG 57, 507–510.
13. *Catechism of the Catholic Church,* n. 1397.
14. *Teachings of Paul VI*, VII (1969). Vatican City: 1970, p. 1130.

- The *bread of unity* among Christians still divided, journeying to share the same bread and the same cup.

A great host

In concluding, I would like to formulate a dream.

I dream of the Holy See, with all its organisms, as a great host—one bread, offered in spiritual sacrifice in the heart of the Church; as a great Cenacle, with Mary, the Mother of the Body of Christ, and with Peter who exercises his ministry of unity at the service of all people. And with them, all of us as grains of wheat, accepting to be ground by the needs of communion in order to form one body, fully united and fully given as bread for the life of the world, as a sign of hope for humanity. One bread, one body.

O res mirabilis! Nec laudare sufficit!

O wonderful reality! Nothing suffices to praise you!

15
JESUS LIVING IN HIS CHURCH
With You All Days

Dilexit Ecclesiam ("He loved the Church"). These are the words written in large letters on the tomb of the founder of an ecclesial movement of our time.[1] Even in difficult moments, even when this man was tried by his superiors, he knew how to recognize in the Church the Spouse and the Body of Christ. For this reason he loved her.

Instead, many of our contemporaries say, "Christ, yes; the Church, no." They do not see the connection between Jesus and the Church. They do not recognize his presence in it. Yet, what is the Church? What does the Church desire to be, if not the one who manifests the face of the Lord in the midst of the world?

The Curé of Ars, that simple and most humble pastor, comes to mind. Called to give testimony about him, a farmer said, "I saw God in a man."

Also, there comes to mind Mother Teresa of Calcutta, and the immense crowd that followed her mortal remains on the day of her funeral. Christians, Hindus, and Moslems alike saw in her the fascination of Jesus.

These great witnesses of the presence of Christ are so precious, and we have to be grateful to the Lord for them. In our time, however, very complex and in need of salvation, it

---

1. Father Joseph Kentenich († 1968), founder of *Opera di Schönstatt*.

is urgent that within the entire Church Christ is seen, and that everyone in the Church radiates his presence.

With his recent continental Synods, John Paul II wanted to underscore this urgency. As a leitmotif during all the Synodal Assemblies was this idea: the living Christ—*Jesus vivens in Ecclesia sua* ("Jesus living in his Church").

How is Jesus present in the Church?

Drawing from the centuries-old tradition of the Church, the Second Vatican Council brought to light the different ways that Christ is present in the Church.[2]

- Jesus is present in the Church in a special way in her liturgical actions, in the person of the minister, and above all in the Eucharistic species.
- Jesus is present with his power in the sacraments.
- Jesus is present in his Word.
- Jesus is present when the Church carries out the works of mercy; he is present in the poor, in the sick, in prisoners (cf. Mt 25:31–46).
- Jesus is present "in the lives of those who, sharing in our humanity, are, however, more perfectly transformed into the image of Christ (cf. 2 Cor 3:18); God vividly manifests his presence and his face to men and women. He speaks to us in them, and gives us a sign of his kingdom."[3]
- Jesus is present in a Christian community that lives in love (cf. Acts 2:42–48; 4:32–35).

Jesus *is* present, though it may often seem that he is not. What happens for many of our contemporaries, and for many

---

2. Cf. Second Vatican Council, *Sacrosanctum Concilium* (Constitution on the Sacred Liturgy)*,* n. 7; *Catechism of the Catholic Church,* n. 1373.

3. *Lumen Gentium* (Dogmatic Constitution on the Church), n. 50.

Christians as well, is what happened to the two disciples of Emmaus. "Jesus himself approached and began to walk with them, but their eyes were kept from recognizing him" (Lk 24:15–16). "He walked along the road as a traveling companion," writes St. Augustine, "in fact, it was he who guided them. Therefore they saw him, but they were not capable of recognizing him. Their eyes, or so we understand, were prevented from recognizing him. They were not prevented from seeing him, but from recognizing him."[4]

"I am in the midst of them"

St. Matthew refers to this promise of Jesus: "For where two or three are gathered in my name, I am there among them" (18:20).

Here we must not think only of the liturgical assembly, but of every situation in which two or more Christians are united in the Spirit, in the love of Jesus. Neither should we think only of the simple omnipresence of the Risen Christ in the entire cosmos.

One exegete of our times has written:

Matthew thinks of a "personalized" presence, so to speak. Jesus is present as the Crucified and Risen One, that is, in that openness of a total self-giving lived on the cross, where he, with all his humanity, opens himself to the divinizing action of the Father and gives himself totally to us communicating to us his spirit, the Holy Spirit. The presence of the Risen One is not, therefore, a static presence, merely a being-here, but a relational presence, a presence that knocks on the door of the heart...it is a presence that gathers and unites, and as a consequence, expects our response, which is faith. In

4. *Discorso 235*, 2: PL 38, 1118.

short, the closeness of Christ gathers "the dispersed sons of God" to make them the Church.[5]

From the moment the Covenant is concluded with Israel on Sinai, Yahweh reveals himself as the One who efficaciously intervenes in history. He liberated the Hebrews from their slavery in Egypt and made them his people. "I am in your midst" are the words that already distinguish that first Covenant: a presence that protects, guides, consoles, and punishes....

With the coming of the New Testament, this presence acquires a completely new and particular intensity. In the resurrection of Jesus, the promise of the definitive presence of God, the promise of the definitive Covenant, finds its fulfillment.

In the Christian community, Emmanuel, that is, God-with-us, is "the savior of his Body," the Church (cf. Eph 5:23). Present in the midst of his own, he convokes and gathers not only Israel, but also all of humanity (cf. Mt 28:19–20). To live with Jesus "in our midst," according to the promise of Matthew 18:20, means to realize even now God's plan for the whole of history and humanity.

A response: in lived communion

How is the permanent presence of the Risen One made visible?

After the collapse of the Berlin Wall, the first Special Assembly of European Bishops gathered to question themselves about the new evangelization of the continent. A Hungarian religious emphasized that the only Bible read by the unchurched "from a distance," so to speak, is the life of

---

5. Gérard Rossé, "*Gesù in mezzo*" *in prospettiva ecclesiale,* in: "Gen's," 30 (2000), pp. 3–4.

Christians. We can also add that we ourselves, our lives, are the only eucharist on which the world of non-Christians can feed.

By the grace of Baptism and particularly through the Eucharist, we are inserted into Christ, but it is in a lived communion that the presence of Jesus manifests itself and becomes operative in everyday existence.

In silence two or three believers can witness in mutual love to what constitutes their profound identity: to be Church in the care of the weakest, in fraternal correction, in common prayer, in forgiveness without limits. St. Paul says: "Walk in love, just as Christ loved us and gave himself up for us to God as an offering and sacrifice with a pleasing fragrance" (Eph 5:2).

We find this orientation in the so-called "missionary mandate of the fourth Gospel": "All will know by this that you are my disciples, if you have love for one another" (Jn 13:35). Where there is reciprocal love, there *one sees* Christ, and the measure of reciprocal love is this: "Greater love than this no man has—to lay down his life for his friends" (Jn 15:13). For this reason, therefore, the *Instrumentum Laboris* of the recent Assembly of the Synod of Bishops in Europe rightly affirms: "If the Eucharist is the greatest presence of the Risen Lord, reciprocal love lived with evangelical radicality is the most transparent presence that most questions and induces one to believe" (n. 45). *Ubi caritas est vera, Deus ibi est* ("where there is true charity, there is God"), proclaims the ancient hymn.

Living members everywhere

In my country before *Perestroika (Dõi Mói),* in each of the two dioceses of Lang Sỏn and Bắc Ninh in North Vietnam, only two priests were left, and they could not freely leave their residences. Cardinal Giuse Maria Trịnh Như Khuê recounts: "Small groups of two or more lived the Gospel daily and helped one another in every way; and in their reciprocal gift they experienced the presence of the One who said, 'But take courage; I have conquered the world!' (Jn 16:33) "

Above all, it is thanks to these small groups, experiencing and witnessing daily to the presence of Christ, that the Church in my country survived. *Everywhere*, in fact, one could verify the presence of Christ, even among two Christians who met in the market or among two men who worked side by side in a re-education camp. It was not necessary to speak to each other. A particular context was not needed. It was enough to be united "in his name," which means in his love. One experienced the presence of the Risen One who enlightens and comforts.

With the presence of Christ in our midst we found hope, that hope which "does not disappoint" (cf. Rom 5:5). Thanks to this, we radiated the Gospel around us. Precisely when all was lost, Jesus began to walk the streets of our country again. He left the tabernacle and made himself present in the schools and in the factories, in the offices and in the prisons.

What distinguishes us

Jesus lives in his Church, and we can come to ask ourselves: is this not a great light especially for us who live and work in the Roman Curia? Do we not find here what, more than anything else, can dispose hearts to listen to us and love us? Without the witness of mutual love, without the living presence of Christ among us—not only in our churches and chapels, but in our offices as well—our work would be like that of a business.

There are approximately 3,500 workers in the Vatican.

But what distinguishes us from any other government organization? The religious functions? Is it the fact that we are dealing with the things of the Church? What can give weight to our actions in the world? "By this will everyone know that you are my disciples: if you have love for one another!"

Certainly, this living presence of Christ in the mutuality of love requires a great purity and nobility of intention.

St. John Chrysostom points out:

> What then? Are there not perhaps two or three gathered in his name? There are, yes, but rarely. In fact, [Jesus] is not speaking simply of a [material] gathering…. What he says has this meaning: if one keeps me as the principal motive of his love toward his neighbor, I will be with him…. Today instead, we see that the major part of humanity has other motivations for their friendships: one loves because he is loved; another because he is honored; another because someone is useful to him…. But it is difficult to find someone who loves for Christ, as one should love one's neighbor…. One who loves this way…even if he is hated, insulted, threatened with death—continues to love…. For this is how Christ loved his enemies…with the greatest love.[6]

It is also St. John Chrysostom who offers us the example of Peter and John according to the account in Acts 3:1:

> Seek to learn how great was their love, their harmony, and their agreement. How they would communicate all and do all united by that bond of friendship in God, and how they appeared together at table, at prayer, in walking, and in every other action. Peter and John were such [that is, united] and had Jesus in their midst. Do you understand how important it is to be united?[7]

---

6. *In Mt. Hom.*, 61, 2–3: PG 58, 587.

7. *In Act. Apost.*, 2, 4: PG 51, 83.

What matters most

The Christian vocation is to live unity.

The Christian community united in mutual love is the actual place where Jesus makes himself visible.

The Christian originality is manifested where two or three are united to rejoice in the presence of the Risen Christ.

Let us ask the grace, dear brothers, that this Jubilee may clothe us in a new love, in renewed harmony and friendship and in a great forbearance, so that the presence of Christ may shine in our midst!

> If we are united, Jesus is among us. And this is enough. It is worth more than any other treasure that our heart can possess: more than mother, father, siblings, or children. It is worth more than a house, work, property; more than the works of art of a great city like Rome. Jesus in our midst is worth more than magnificent monuments, sumptuous mausoleums, or all the splendors of the Vatican; more than our soul! [8]

Many years ago, the Holy Father, Paul VI, in speaking with Chiara Lubich, saw precisely in this conviction the true wealth of the Church.

---

8. Cf. C. Lubich, *Scritti Spirituali 3,* Rome: 1979, p. 176.

16

Icon of the Trinity

Your Hope Is the Church

Perhaps in no other place than in Rome can we be so aware of the Church's catholicity and of its mystery of communion.

At this moment, I see the spaces of this chapel enlarging themselves, and I feel the Church throbbing in the different points of the earth. I feel it living around the tabernacles in villages lost in the Amazon and in Central Africa where, around the Eucharistic Jesus, lives his mystical Body. I feel it throbbing in the heart of the great metropolitan cities of the United States and Europe. A few faithful are enough, united in faith and in mutual love, to make the Church present and alive.

I feel a passionate love whenever I contemplate the Church. I would like to share this love with you. Are we not here, in the heart of the Church where Peter placed his See, precisely to love it more and to be at its service?

We are sons of the Church

We love this Church, of which we feel ourselves to be living members. We want to repeat from the depth of our hearts, as Teresa of Avila: "We are 'sons' of the Church!"[1]

---

1. The exact words, "I am a daughter of the Church," were the last words spoken by the saint on her deathbed.

We love the Church because:

She has grafted us, this pure Mother, into her family,
opening for us the doors of the true Paradise
    through the priests and the sacraments.

She molds us into soldiers of Christ.

She has pardoned and cancelled our sins
    seventy times seven times.

She has nourished us with the Body of Jesus:
    has divinely sealed the love of our father
    and our mother.

She has raised poor people like us to a high dignity,
    and has invested us with the priesthood.

At the end, she will give a last goodbye to God.
She will give us God.

If our heart does not sing of her, it is a dead organ.

If our mind does not see and admire her, it is blind
    and gloomy.

If our mouth does not speak of her, it is better
    that the word dries up in us.[2]

The beauty of the early Church

In the isolation of my prison cell, I often thought of the Acts of the Apostles, that "Gospel of the Holy Spirit," which gave me great incentive to be in communion with the whole Church.

Those who came to the faith, recounts the Acts, "devoted themselves to the teaching of the apostles and to the fellowship, to the breaking of the bread and to prayer.... All the believers were together and had everything in common..." (Acts 2:42, 44).

---

2. C. Lubich, *L'Attrattiva del Tempo Moderno, Scritti Spirituali 1*, Rome: 1991, pp. 217–218.

In the light of this testimony of the early Church, we can distinguish three aspects of ecclesial communion:

1. Faithful adherence to the Apostles and to their teaching.

2. Participation in the *koinonia* of the three Divine Persons.

3. The fraternal communion that derives from it.

I would like to dedicate a word to each of these three dimensions.

1. The Church is communion because it adheres to the Apostles and to their teaching.

As witnesses to the incarnation, death, and resurrection of Jesus, the Apostles are indispensable intermediaries between Christ and the faithful. Certainly, everyone can also have a direct relationship with Christ, but that still requires previous knowledge of Jesus through the witness of the Apostles and of those who continue their work.

Therefore, without complete adherence to the Apostles, communion with Christ is not possible—at least not in the full and total sense. For this reason, Acts speaks of a diligence to the teachings of the Apostles. It strongly insists on the announcement of the Word, which from the beginning of the Church unfolded according to the three types of teaching and preaching that still exist today. These are *kerygma* or evangelization; *catechesis* or, rather, teaching in the real and true sense; and finally, the *homily*, which is connected to liturgical celebrations and especially to the Eucharist.

In a word, without "the obedience of faith," without the Holy Spirit "moving the heart and turning it to God, opening the eyes of the mind and giving 'joy and ease to everyone in assenting to the truth and believing in it'" (*Dei Verbum*, n. 5), there is no ecclesial communion in the sense of the *et unam, sanctam, catholicam et apostolicam ecclesiam* ("one, holy, catholic, and apostolic church") that we confess in the Creed.

This has been experienced many times in my country. Unity with the teaching of the Church was our salvation.

2. The Church is communion because it participates in the life of the three Divine Persons.

If Christians are united among themselves, it is not simply because they have only one thought, that of Jesus and that of the Apostles, or merely because they are of "one heart and mind" (cf. Acts 4:32). Above all, they are united because they participate in the unity of the Father, the Son, and the Holy Spirit (cf. Jn 17:21–24); because they are united to Christ (cf. 1 Cor 10:16, a clear allusion to the Eucharist); because they share in the sufferings of Christ (cf. 1 Pet 4:13); and because they are united in the Spirit (cf. 2 Cor 13:13).

The Second Vatican Council helped us to grasp, with greater awareness, the Church as a mystery of communion. As the Extraordinary Synod of 1985 underlined in its final document, the reality of *communion* constitutes the central and fundamental ecclesiological idea of Vatican II. To speak of Church-communion, the conciliar teaching goes directly to the source: the Church is communion and unity because it is, as St. Cyprian says: "people gathered in the unity of the Father, and of the Son, and of the Holy Spirit" (cf. *Lumen Gentium,* n. 4). The Church is the *Church of the Trinity*—its icon, that is, its image and participation; and everything in the Church is a reflection of the Trinity and finds its model in the trinitarian communion.

Here is the key for interpreting and authentically living all ecclesial relationships. We know that the three Divine Persons live in the fullest reciprocal self-giving: *one with the other, one for the other, one in the other*. In living the new commandment of Jesus, the Church lives according to this supreme model.

The nature of Church-communion leads us to live in a

"trinitarian" relationship also on the social plane. It means not only mutual love between persons, but between bishops, between priests, between religious, between the different Orders, between groups and movements. It means mutual love to the point of loving another's diocese as one's own, one's dicastery as that of the other, the charism of the other as one's own; to the point of enfolding all of humanity in this reciprocal love so that one loves the country of another as one's own, the culture of another as one's own; to the point of realizing the prayer of Jesus: "Father...that they all may be one as you and I are one."

Sad to say, this fullness of communion is often lacking. This is, in a certain sense, worse than a Nazi or communist persecution, since this is an attack on the Church that comes, not from without, but from within. Where communion is lacking, large, cancerous cells are created in the heart of the Church. It is enough to consider how, in a diocese where there is no communion among the priests, a bishop is forced to dedicate more time in resolving internal problems than in carrying out evangelization projects and preventing external difficulties.

3. The Church is fraternal communion of spiritual and material goods.

According to the testimony of Acts, the communion of Christians—as I have already mentioned in the meditation on the Eucharist—must ultimately result in a certain sharing of material goods. This sharing should not be only within a single community, but also among the different churches. Acts mentions the existence of other communities: that of Jerusalem in Judea; those in Galilee, in Samaria (Acts 9:31); at Damascus (9:2–8, 19–25); and in Antioch (11:19–21). From the very beginning, the communion among the churches takes the form of a "collection" to help the most poor, such as those of Jerusalem (cf. Acts 11:29–30; 2 Cor 8:1–9, 15). This is also manifested under the form of hospitality (cf. Acts 10:6 and 48). In these concrete expressions, St. Luke sees this willingness to share as inspired by those profound spiritual ties which unite the members of the early community.

I would like to recall here an experience I had many years ago. In 1954, Bishop Hans Daneels of Cologne was sent by the German Episcopal Conference to Vietnam to help the refugees. In 1957, I went to Cologne to visit him. As I traveled, seeing the destruction of the war still evident, I asked him, "Why are you helping us when your own country is still under reconstruction?" He answered, "This is help from the poor to the poorer." I understood this to be true communion.

Communion and mission

The *Church of the Trinity* is therefore, in its essence, a mystery of communion in the reality of space and time. In this way, it becomes the instrument for carrying out God's plan for all creation: to unify all things in Christ and in trinitarian unity (cf. *Lumen Gentium,* n. 1). "Communion begets communion, essentially it is likened to a mission on behalf of communion," says *Christifideles Laici*. The Holy Father explains:

> Communion and mission are profoundly connected with each other, they interpenetrate and mutually imply each other to the point that communion represents both the source and the fruit of mission: communion gives rise to mission and mission is accomplished in communion (n. 32).

From this arises the immediate consequence of evangelization. Addressing the clerics of Rome on March 1, 1990, John Paul II said:

We have to be in very profound communion with God
in order to bring forward his mission of communion, his
divine, trinitarian mission. We have to be always more
in communion among ourselves, united among ourselves, because this is the consequence of our similar-
ity—we are the image and likeness of God—of our
Christian vocation. This is also an imperative of evangelical, missionary, and pastoral strategy.[3]

At the service of the unity of the Church

Let us look at ourselves within this Church, which is at
the same time both communion and mission.

As members of the Church, we are also called to be
servants of the Church. We live of the Church and for the
Church. We are ready to give our life for the Church as were
Paul of Tarsus, Ignatius of Antioch, Augustine of Hippo, and
all the Fathers of the Church. Members of the Church, we are
called to become fathers and mothers of the Church. How can
we be apostles, martyrs, confessors, and doctors? Therese of
the Child Jesus says: "In the heart of the Church, my Mother,
I will be love,"[4] because—and these are her words—Jesus
"does not in fact need our works, but only our love."[5]

In this Church-communion, our particular way of being
love expresses itself in the ministry of the Roman Curia. Here
we are dealing with real service, a *diakonia* according to the
model of Christ himself who "did not come to be served, but
to serve and to give his own life as a ransom for the many"
(cf. Mk 10:45). "It is necessary therefore," says the Constitution *Pastor Bonus*, "to understand and exercise the power of
the Church according to the categories of service" (n. 2), in

---

3. *Teachings of John Paul II*, XIII, 1, Cittá del Vaticano: 1992, p. 566.
4. *Manuscrit Autobiographique B*, 3 v.
5. Ibid., 1 v.

order that "communion may be established always more, may have vigor, and continue to produce its marvelous fruits" (n. 1).

A very concrete area in which we can carry out our particular ministry of communion is, without a doubt, the welcoming of bishops on their *ad limina* visits. The *ad limina* visits, we read in *Pastor Bonus*, should result in "a particular moment of that communion which determines so profoundly the substance of the Church" (n. 5).

How can we not linger here to take note that our *diakonia* especially requires a communion among ourselves? Even for us as individuals and as offices and dicasteries, the model is the Trinity. Like the entire Church, and for even stronger reasons, we are asked to live *one with the other, one for the other, one in the other*. Then, the bishops coming from the various continents will find a "community," a "permanent cenacle."

The apple of one's eye

In his book *Gift and Mystery*, John Paul II tells of how, as a young priest, he was counseled to go to the Eternal City not only to study, but also to "learn Rome itself."[6] And at the heart of this Rome is the Roman Curia.

During the years in my dicastery, I have not only received diplomats but also numerous groups of priests, seminarians, laity, adults, and young people who came from far away and who wanted to know the work of the Roman Curia. I have not, however, had much contact with the ecclesiastical students who have the fortune of being able to form themselves in the capital of Christianity and who are "the apple of the eye" of St. Peter and of the successors of the Apostles. Often,

---

6. John Paul II, *Dono e Mistero. Nel 50ᵗʰ del Mio Sacerdozio.* Libreria Editrice Vaticana, 1996, p. 60.

they do not know the Curia except through the newspapers. How can they love and cooperate with the Curia in the future, if they do not know it from close up today?

While pondering the formation of priests, religious, and laity in the center of the universal Church, it seems to me very important and even essential that we find a way to give everyone—at least once during their stay—the opportunity for a deeper contact with the Roman Curia. They can get a degree anywhere, but not the "Roman experience."

How a little fish can bring hope

I would like to conclude this meditation with a very simple experience, as always from the time of my imprisonment.

It is difficult to imagine with how much anxiety our faithful in Vietnam—during the years of greatest trial (from 1958 onward)—defying threats of punishment or imprisonment for listening to "foreign and reactionary propaganda," tuned in to *Vatican Radio* in order to hear the heartbeat of the universal Church and be united with the successor of Peter.

Much later, I encountered similar circumstances.

I was in isolation in Hanoi when one day, a policewoman brought a small fish for me to cook. As soon as I saw the wrappings, I immediately felt a start of joy, but I was careful not to show this externally. My happiness was not because of the fish, but because of the pages of newspaper in which it was wrapped: two pages of the *L'Osservatore Romano*. At that time, when the Vatican newspaper arrived at the post office in Hanoi, it was often confiscated and sold at the market as paper. Those two pages had been used to wrap the little fish. Calmly, without bringing attention to myself, I washed those sheets of newspaper to remove the smell, and then dried them in the sun and preserved them as a relic.

For me, in that unbroken regime of isolation, those pages were a sign of communion with Rome, with Peter, with the Church, and an embrace from Rome. I would not have been able to survive without an awareness of being part of the Church.

Today we live in a world that rejects the values of the civilization of life, of love, and of truth; our hope is the Church, *Image of the Trinity*.

17

You Are in Me and I Am in You
To Live in Communion

In 1995, John Paul II addressed a sizable group of bishops including me, saying, "The Lord Jesus did not call the disciples to an individual following, but one inseparably personal and communitarian. If this is true for all the baptized, it is valid in a particular way for the Apostles and for their successors."[1]

I am convinced that this new millennium requires a communitarian life that is conspicuously ecclesial, and especially from those who have tasks of responsibility in the Church.

At the dawn of monasticism

I would like to invite you to return to the first millennium for a moment.

"Flee from men, and you will be saved," advised an anchorite in the desert of Egypt. And again: "I cannot be at the same time with God and with men."[2] Confronted with a frivolous and extravagant world, retiring into solitude to be with God seemed the only way to follow Jesus without reserve in

---

1. *Teachings of John Paul II,* XVIII, 1 (1995). Cittá del Vaticano: 1997, p. 382.
2. PG 31, 931–934.

that age. This conviction marked the history of Christianity for centuries. The *Imitation of Christ* affirms: "When they could, the greatest saints avoided the company of men, and preferred to serve God in solitude. A wise man said, 'Every time I go among men, I return less a man….' Instead, the one who distances himself from friends and acquaintances, draws near to God and his angels."[3]

Nothing, in effect, can equal those moments when the soul, leaving everything behind, finds itself immersed in a profound one-on-one dialogue with God.

Yet, the Desert Fathers soon realized that the Gospel could not be fully lived if not lived together. Basil the Great writes:

> Our Creator wanted us to have need of one another precisely so that we would live in unity with one another…. In fact, if you live alone, whose feet can you wash? Whom can you care for? How can you put yourself in the last place? Communitarian life is, therefore, a stadium where we exercise as athletes, a gymnasium that makes us progress, a continual exercise of perfection in the commandments of God.[4]

The Cenobites would be born of this conviction of the necessity of living the Gospel together and enjoying the permanent presence of Christ.

A new Pentecost

In my opinion, we are living an analogous and marvelous evolution today. In the last few centuries, strong emphasis was placed on the value of the individual. So, too, in the spiritual life. But for some decades now, the communitarian

---

3. Lib. I, c. 20, 1–6.
4. *Regulae Fusius Tractatae*, Interrogazione 7, 3, 1–2: PG 31, 928–929.

dimension has been reinvigorated among the People of God. This is the Church "reawakened in the soul," as Romano Guardini has said. Under the breath of the Spirit there opens before us a new way that has its fulcrum in *koinonia*—communion!

"We older ones," Karl Rahner wrote years ago, "given our background and our formation, were spiritually individualistic." He maintained that in the future, a spirituality lived *together* would have a determining role. As confirmation of this, he cited the experience of the first Pentecost: "an event—one must presume—that certainly did not consist in a casual gathering of a number of individualistic mystics, but in the experience of the Spirit created by the community."[5]

It is necessary to return joyfully to the style of Christian life at its highest charismatic moment: Pentecost. Sweetly, but decidedly, the Spirit invites us to live communion not only as a gift, but also as a response and an adherence on our part; to live communion not only as a spiritual participation in the mystery of the One and Triune God, but also as a concrete interpersonal communion. Thus will be realized the *new Pentecost of the Church,* often referred to by the last few Popes.

Unity: a sign of the times

Let us look around ourselves to grasp even more the urgency of a true life of communion!

The world itself is moving toward unity, and this is accented by multiple signs.

The international organizations born after the Second World War were an attempt at creating a worldwide composition. Science, technology, cultural and commercial exchange,

---

5. K. Rahner, *Elementi di Spiritualità nella Chiesa del Futuro*, in: T. Goffi—B. Secondin (a cura di), *Problemi e Prospettive de Spiritualita.* Brescia: 1983, pp. 440–441.

the ease of travel, sports events, the mass media including the present internet explosion, are all factors that draw people together and promote encounters between individuals and cultures. In its political, economic, and social structures, today's world appears connected by an organic and profound interdependence.

Sad to say, many times this straining toward unity arrives on the tail end of globalization and is guided solely by special interests. While on the one hand there are grandiose overall designs for globalization, on the other hand millions and billions of people remain excluded.

It is as if from humanity and from the Church of today there arises an appeal, almost a cry, that calls for globalization of another kind, one not guided by the logic of profit but by the law of love. Certainly, the Holy Spirit has placed this yearning in the hearts of today's men and women. And the Spirit pushes the Church to become communion in such a way as to respond to humanity's longing.

"Our times demand a new evangelization," said the Pope in the same discourse cited at the beginning of this meditation. And he also specifies some conditions: *"A renewed proclamation of the Gospel cannot be consistent and efficacious if it is not accompanied by a robust spirituality of communion...."*[6]

How to live communion in our time

Let us seek to understand what is new about a "robust spirituality of communion."

I think it consists in the awareness that fraternal communion, when it is based on the Gospel, is the privileged place of

6. *Teachings of John Paul II*, XVIII, 1, (1995). Cittá del Vaticano: 1997, p. 382.

encounter with God. This is one of the fundamental themes in the Johannine writings: "No one has ever seen God, but if we love one another God *remains in us* and his love is made perfect in us" (1 Jn 4:12).

I am convinced that in our times the Holy Spirit has sown new spiritual and communitarian charisms, suitable for accomplishing a renewal of the Christian life in this sense.

Many years ago I came across a text that really struck me as an expression of this new vision, inspired by the relationship of trinitarian communion:

> God who is in me, who has formed my soul in which the Trinity reposes (with the saints and with the angels), is also in the hearts of my brothers and sisters. It is not reasonable that I love him only in myself.
>
> Therefore, our cell (as a soul intimate with God would say) is in us: my heaven is in me, and just *as* it is in me, it is in the souls of others....
>
> Thus, it is necessary always to assemble also in the presence of one's brother, but not avoiding the creature—on the contrary, perceiving him in your own heaven or perceiving yourself in his heaven.[7]

Here is the novelty: the other person is not an *obstacle* to holiness, but is the *way* to holiness. Rather than avoiding him or her in order to find intimacy with God, it is a matter of seeking him or her in order to create together that "theological space in which one can experience the mystical presence of the Risen Lord."[8]

---

7. J. M. Povilus, *"Gesù in Mezzo" nel Pensiero di Chiara Lubich,* Rome: 1981, p. 73.

8. John Paul II, *Apostolic Exhortation Vita Consecrata* (Consecrated Life). Boston: Pauline Books & Media, 1996, n. 42.

Concrete dimensions

We seek to illustrate, through three examples, what this awareness involves in our life.

1. Asceticism in daily life

From my father, who was a builder, I learned that to construct a house with reinforced concrete, you must purify all the elements well: the iron, the sand, the gravel, and the cement. The strength of the building you construct depends upon this work of purification to eliminate all impure elements.

This is similar to what happens regarding communion among us. To know how to go against oneself, to mortify oneself, is indispensable. Various practices, such as fasting, exist for this purpose. However, the most evangelical and at the same time most accessible practice, possible at every moment, is one's relationship with one's neighbor. To welcome the other, to be always available, to know how to listen, how to be patient, to make oneself all to all, to put the interests of others before one's own, is a continual renunciation and places us in God.

While I was in prison, I wrote:

Communion is a battle of every instant.
Even one moment of neglect can shatter it;
a trifle is enough;
a single thought against charity,
an obstinately held judgment,
a sentimental attachment,
a mistaken premise,
ambition or personal interest,
an action done for self and not for the Lord....

Help me, Lord, to examine myself in this way:
What is the center of my life?
You or me?

If it is you, you will gather us in unity.
But if I see around me
everyone gradually leaving and dispersing,
this is the sign that I have put myself at the center.[9]

2. Substantial prayer

All of the spiritual masters teach us how to pray: it is necessary to prepare oneself, to recollect oneself, and to know how to go deep. At times, however, our prayer is dry. Our celebrations risk becoming little more than a pious habit. Jesus gives us a word to indicate the true way: "If you are presenting your offering at the altar and remember there that your brother has something against you...first go be reconciled to your brother, and then you can come and make your offering" (Mt 5:23–24).

Everyone has experienced to some degree how, after a profound encounter with our neighbor, after re-establishing a full and cordial understanding with the people we live or work with, prayer flows spontaneously from the heart, and the Holy Mass acquires a particular intensity.

Without communion among ourselves, our prayer does not please God. In fact, how can he remain in our soul if we are divided, he who *is* unity?

3. Not only silence, but also the word and sharing

There is yet another expression of a spiritual life lived in communion, and it is particularly important. In our formation, we learned the value of *silence* in order to listen well to the voice of God in our own hearts. Yet, no less essential is the *word*, to share one's own spiritual experience with others in

---

9. *Preghiere di Speranza. Tredici Anni in Carcere,* Cinisello Balsamo, 1997, pp. 44–45.

simplicity. At times, I marvel to see how seldom we in the Church speak of our personal experience of God.

According to St. Ignatius of Loyola, such a lack of communication is a weapon of the devil.

> Seeing the servant of the Lord so good and humble who, while accomplishing the will of God, thinks that he is completely useless.... The devil makes this person believe that if he speaks of some grace given to him by God our Lord, of works, resolutions, and desires, he sins with another kind of vainglory because he is speaking of his own honor. The devil tries to make the person not speak of the benefits received from the Lord, thus impeding the yield of fruit in others and in himself given that the remembrance of benefits received always fosters greater things.[10]

St. Lawrence Justinian writes in turn:

> Nothing in the world gives more praise to God and reveals him as more worthy of praise than the humble and fraternal sharing of spiritual gifts: such gifts invigorate charity, since they cannot flourish in solitude.... It is...a precept of the Lord to exercise this virtue always, by means of word and action, toward our brothers. Thus, if you do not want to be transgressors of his law and be judged as souls who nonchalantly disdain the salvation of the brothers, having received so many graces from heaven, let them study with all diligence how to pour out on others those divine graces that have been communicated to them, especially the gifts that can help them on the way of perfection.[11]

---

10. Letter of June 18, 1537, in: *Gli Scritti di Ignazio di Loyola. Epistolario.* Turin: 1977, pp. 725–726.

11. *Disciplina e Perfezione della Vita Monastica.* Rome: 1967, p. 4.

To build the Church

We come now to look at the Scriptures.

Did not Jesus give rise to the new People of God, communicating to the disciples all the words of his Father?

Did not Mary, perhaps, tell of her most intimate experience when she sang her *Magnificat*?

Did not Paul build up his communities by communicating what he was living? He told everything about himself—his conversion, his journeys as an apostle, even the most profound experiences such as his rapture to the third heaven and his mystical relationship with Christ. He even shared the anguish that gripped him at the thought of his people not accepting the revelation of Christ, as well as his own weaknesses, trials, and the thorn in the flesh. We can say that he communicated his soul and his life to others, and thus he built up the Church.

In my country, since every type of Catholic association is forbidden, the people concentrate completely on the Word of God. Not having spiritual books in print, they communicate the fruits of living the Word among themselves. They have only the Gospel and the reciprocal communication of what they live. Even with this reduction to the very essentials, Christian life flourishes.

When, instead, an Episcopal Conference is divided—as happened in some countries under Communist rule—it loses credibility in the eyes of the people. Some bishops from East-Central Europe spoke to me about this in the 1970s. In such cases, the only thing that remains is a community of bishops living side by side without that communion which unites Jesus to the Father.

The "exterior castle"

St. Teresa of Avila, a doctor of the Church, speaks of a splendid and luminous "interior castle." This is the reality of the soul inhabited by the Most Holy Trinity; a reality to discover inside ourselves, that animates all of life and leads to perfect union with God and to service of our neighbor.

In this age of globalization, in this hour of Church-communion, has the moment perhaps arrived—as already observed—to discover, to illuminate, to build up the "exterior castle"[12] in addition to the "interior castle"? In other words, the presence of God is not only in us, but also among us. This is the castle of two or more united in the name of the Lord. It is the castle never demolished, but continuously built up and preserved in every relationship, to the point of reaching the splendor of perfect unity.

St. Augustine writes: "We form together the house of the Lord, but only if we are mutually united in love."[13] "We are his temple both collectively and individually. He desires to live in union with all and with each person."[14]

I dream of the Church of the Third Millennium as a House that guards the presence of the living God. A Holy City that descends from on high, not as a collection of loose stones, but as a well-made and harmonious construction, rendered solid by a lived communion. I dream of this City, which guards at its center the Lamb as the source of light for all humanity.

---

12. Cf. C. Lubich, *La Spiritualità Collettiva e i Suoi Strumenti,* in: "Gen's," 25, 1995, p. 52.

13. *Discorso 336,* 1, 1: PL 37, 1736.

14. St. Augustine, *The City of God,* 10, 3, 2: PL 41, 280.

To Renew the Hope Within Us

18

Little Flock

Do Not Be Afraid

In the recent Special Assembly of the Synod of Bishops for Europe, the Synodal Fathers repeatedly emphasized that today the Church in traditionally Christian lands finds itself a "minority." They indicated as some prominent reasons the drop in priestly and religious vocations, the decrease in religious practice, the confinement of religion to the private sphere with the related difficulty of influencing customs and institutions, and the problem of transmitting the faith to new generations. A bishop confided to me that at one time, he had 145 seminarians, but last year only one young man entered the seminary. Another told me, "I have been a bishop for seven years. I have ordained seven priests and I have buried 147."

Elsewhere, thanks be to God, there are vocations, but admission to the seminary is sometimes limited by the government, and each year only five seminarians can be accepted per diocese. In certain countries, the bishops must remain in office until 80 and even 90 years of age, because the government will not give its approval for a successor. In other countries, due to multiple difficulties, Christians immigrate to the West, and the lands that were Christian from apostolic times have become "museums of the Christian era." In still other areas of the world, only one priest, who is often physically and spiritually exhausted from long journeys under the tropical sun, ministers to thirty communities.

To be in the minority is, in effect, a characteristic of the life of the Church in our day.

Where is the Vatican?

I travel with a diplomatic passport from the Holy See and I frequently run into difficulties from airport police. In general, the Italians do not cause any problems, but it can happen that they may make me wait because they want to show my passport to their co-workers. In Germany, it is more difficult. "What is the Holy See?" they ask. They are amazed by the fact that the Holy See can issue passports. It is still more difficult in Malaysia. "Where is the Holy See? Where is the Vatican?" they ask me. To my response, "In Italy, in Rome," they lead me to a large map. "Show me Italy… And Rome… And where do you find the Vatican?" But the Vatican is not on the map. So I have to wait a half-hour with the illegal immigrants. In the end, the head of the police says to his subordinates: "*I know. The Vatican is a former French colony!*"

The mystery of the minority

Let us turn our attention again to the history of the People of God, to Sacred Scripture, to identify stories and facts that can shed light on our situation as a "minority."

The Bible refers to many situations in which God is served by the weak in order to confound the strong. From a condition of inferiority, Moses prevailed over Pharaoh and liberated his people; Judith overcame Holofernes; Esther, Haman.

In the history of the Church, there is no lack of examples. Catherine of Siena, a woman with no power, succeeded in bringing the Pope back from Avignon to Rome. Don Bosco's counsel was sought by both the Pope and the king.

When, every Good Friday at the Colosseum, we see the Pope carrying the cross, we have before our eyes the "mystery of the minority"—this cross that conquered the great colossus of Imperial Rome.

"How many divisions does the Pope have?" (*Joseph Stalin*)

From the aspect of a "quantitative minority," I would like to reflect on the surprising story of Gideon, a charismatic leader of Israel in the twelfth century before Christ.

The seventh chapter of the Book of Judges relates how Gideon prepared himself for the battle against Midian. "The troops with you are too many for me to give the Midianites into their hand," the Lord said to him. Then God explains, "Israel would only take the credit away from me, saying, 'My own hand has delivered me'" (v. 2).

Therefore, according to the Lord's directives, Gideon reduced the troops from 32,000 men to 10,000 and then from 10,000 to just 300. These 300 men, armed only with horns and clay jars with torches inside, invaded the enemy camp making a tremendous racket. Then, "when they blew the 300 trumpets, the Lord set every man's sword against his fellow and against all the army" (v. 22).

Some spontaneous considerations arise:

Like the people of the Old Covenant at the time of Gideon, so also today, the new Israel must confront many forces which make progress through an abuse of their power. It is necessary to react, but like Israel, a Church that is too powerful runs the risk of bragging about itself, of falling into triumphalism, of attributing success to itself.

This makes us think how those "weapons," seemingly so ridiculous, were suddenly able to produce an incredible effect. In the same way as Gideon, a Church that completely abandons itself to the mandate of the Lord can obtain important results without great means. A trumpet is enough to announce the Word of the Lord and a torch the light of God, on the condition that we are broken vessels.

As it happened at Midian, so it can happen today that the enemy destroys itself, and the Church will not have to exert a great effort to remove itself from difficulties. The ways of evil and injustice end up destroying themselves. Do not let it be said, therefore, that a "reduced number" necessarily annuls the effective strength of the Church.

"You cannot go out against this Philistine" (*King Saul*)

The "qualitative minority" brings us to think of how the Lord has acted in times relatively close to our own. Whether at Lourdes, Fatima, or La Salette, the Blessed Mother did not choose to appear to well prepared or educated people, but to one or more children, to shepherds, to those who were almost ignorant. She has always indicated the same means for confronting difficulties and dangers: prayer and conversion.

However, let us return now to the Scriptures and meditate on the figure of David as an example of a great biblical leader who used modest, humanly inadequate means for his mission.

We all know that the event that suddenly made David known and launched him toward the throne was his victory over the Philistines, and in particular, his duel with the giant, Goliath (cf. 1 Sam 17).

I would like to highlight some details that can help us to grasp the relevance of this story.

The giant who ridiculed David, and who ridicules us, represents evil, or rather, anti-evangelical ideologies and values. Goliath is hostile, threatening, provocative, "Come to me, and I will give your flesh to the birds of the air and to the wild animals of the field" (v. 44).

Even today the Church, confronted with evil, is battling against Goliath, a terrifying giant who seems invincible. Before it, at the first blow, the Church—and with her each of us—experiences a strong sense of powerlessness. And the world does not lack those who feel the need to reinforce this sensation, saying as Saul said, "You are not able to go against this Philistine" (v. 33).

In the beginning, David took the wrong road. He dressed in the armor of power and strength; that is, he followed the way of the world to defend himself (vv. 38–39a). But that paralyzed him. "I cannot walk with these; for I am not used to them," he says (v. 39b). The Church is exactly like this when she has recourse to the world's arsenal.

The fact is, the Church has her own "weapons" to fight with, and these are *the only true weapons* that count. And among them one shines forth. David says, "You come to me with sword and spear and javelin, but I come to you *in the name of the Lord of hosts*" (v. 45). All other weapons are merely accessories (v. 40): the "staff" of violence that David, however, does not use in the battle; then, very simply, a sling and five smooth stones from a stream. Every giant has a weak point. It suffices to look carefully, for a little stone well aimed defeated the giant, and his own sword was used to cut off his head (vv. 41–54).

David is an image of the Church today. In many situations, we are a minority in terms of numbers, strength, possibilities, and means, but just like David, we go forward *in nomine Domini*—in the name of the Lord.

Jesus: the man of few numbers

Now let us to turn our gaze on Jesus.

In Sacred Scripture, Moses represents the man of great numbers. When the Israelites left Egypt, they numbered "about six-hundred-thousand men on foot, besides children." Scripture also tells us that "a mixed crowd went up with them, and livestock in great numbers, both flocks and herds" (cf. Ex 12:37–38).

By comparison, Jesus appears as the man of few numbers. His attention is especially turned toward the "little ones," to sinners, to Zacchaeus, to the Samaritan woman, to the pardoned sinful woman, to the adulteress….

In his teaching about the Reign of God, no grandiose or flashy figures emerge: "What is the kingdom of God like, and to what should I compare it? It is like mustard seed that a man took and threw into his garden, and it grew and became a tree, and the birds of the sky nested in its branches" (Lk 13:18–19).

And again: "To what shall I compare the kingdom of God? It is like yeast that a woman took and mixed into a bushel of wheat flour until all of it was leavened" (Lk 13:20–21).

He said: "This is how the kingdom of God is, like a man who throws seed upon the earth and sleeps and rises by night and day, and the seed sprouts and grows while he is unaware" (Mk 4:26–27).

Jesus does not compare his group of disciples to a squadron prepared to fight or to exult in victory. Rather, he says:

"Fear not, little flock, for it pleased your Father to give you the kingdom" (Lk 12:32).

"You are the salt of the earth, but if the salt should lose its taste, what can it be salted with?" (Mt 5:13)

"You are the light of the world…" (Mt 5:14).

"See, I am sending you out as lambs into the midst of wolves" (Lk 10:3), he says to his own. Then Jesus tells the disciples to go without money and without power, to bring neither knapsack nor walking staff (cf. Mt 10:9–10).

In his parables and in his stories, a few numbers and minute things emerge indicating that his attention is on the individual, on things humble and essential.

He speaks of "two small coins" (that is, a penny) which the widow tossed into the temple treasury (cf. Mk 12:41–42); of the shepherd who left the ninety-nine sheep to go and look for the one that was lost (cf. Lk 15:4–7); of the woman who had ten drachmas and swept the house until she found the one that she had lost (cf. Lk 15:8–10).

Five loaves of bread and two small fish were enough for Jesus to satisfy a vast crowd.

As a "minority" the Church is called to live according to this style of the Gospel, to make her own the priorities and preferences of Jesus.

The wall of the new Jericho

Historically, the Church in her universal and local dimensions was the minority in the presence of Imperial Rome and the barbarian invasions. She was weakened by internal divisions in the modern era, during the French Revolution; and in the century that just ended she suffered from the abuse of Nazism, of Communism, and now from consumerism....

Yet, before the Goliaths of every epoch, the Lord sent defenseless Davids—a Cyril, an Athanasius, a Hilary of Poitiers, an Ambrose and an Augustine, a Francis of Assisi, a Dominic, a Brigid and a Catherine, an Ignatius of Loyola, a Peter Canisius and a Charles Borromeo, a Teresa and a Thomas More; and in our own time, all the great Popes of the twentieth century and shepherds like Wyszynski, Mindszenty, Beran, Stepinac, Tomasek, and Gong Pin Mei.

Paul VI, the Pope lacerated by the post-conciliar crisis, chose as his motto: *in nomine Domini* ("in the name of the

Lord"). From the very beginning of his pontificate, John Paul II has made the cross his emblem, *the one hope*; and Mary, *vita dulcedo et spes nostra* ("our life, our sweetness and our hope"). And he declared: "Do not be afraid! Communism is only a parenthesis in history." Many ridiculed him for this, believing him to be unrealistic. They said the map of the world was already completely red. But the wall of the new Jericho (Berlin) did indeed fall, and the Church has crossed the threshold of the Third Millennium.

Unexpected ways of the Lord

When I was in forced residence in the village of Giang Xá, 20 kilometers from Hanoi, a Catholic man guarded me. At first, he asked me many personal questions: what had this bishop done to be detained in this way? Living and eating with me, sleeping in the room next to mine, he gradually understood. He allowed me to write spiritual books, and brought priests, who traveled distances of 300 kilometers, to hear me talk about the Second Vatican Council, because no North Vietnamese bishop had been able to participate in the Council.

Every month this guard had to prepare a written report about me for the police. He did this for some time, but then he told me:

"I'm not writing anymore. I don't know what to write."

"You have to write! If you don't write, you'll be replaced. A new guard will harm me."

"But I don't know what to write!"

"Then I'll write the report. You copy and sign it."

"Okay."

Later, the police congratulated him on his report, and gave him a bottle of orange liquor as a reward. He brought it to the house and we drank it together in the evening.

Thanks to him, I secretly ordained priests who had been incardinated in other dioceses and sent to me by their bishops. Since I was already in prison, I did not run any risks. By night, the guard would introduce the seminarians to me and they would give me the bishop's ceremonial and the holy oils they brought with them. These were the longest ordinations in the world because they were spread over two days—beginning around 11:30 P.M. and ending the next day at 1:00 A.M.!

This guard even took me to administer the sacraments to the sick. I would never have imagined that Jesus would call me to such an original type of pastoral work. Really, the Holy Spirit can use any kind of person as an instrument of his grace!

The marvels of the Lord

I conclude with two other experiences.

On the island of Zanzibar on the immense Indian Ocean, in a poor village beneath coconut trees, I met two young German ladies, one a doctor and the other a nurse. What were they doing there? They were volunteers who had gone to witness to Christian love in the midst of this Moslem stronghold. A grain of salt in the Ocean! What faith!

At Bagamayo, the port in Eastern Tanzania where the first missionaries had disembarked, I visited the old cemetery of the Spiritan Fathers, near a *baobab*—a colossal tree from Africa. All of the missionaries buried there had died young, the oldest among them died at 39. In silence, I knelt down and kissed the ground: *Mirabilis Dominus in sanctis suis!* ("Wonderful is the Lord in his saints!") And I heard the wind rustling through the coconut leaves: Little flock, do not be afraid.

Therefore: *Do not be afraid! Let us go forward in the name of the Lord!* The walls of the new Jericho will fall.

19

RECEIVE THE HOLY SPIRIT
To Renew the Face of the Earth

Not many years ago on French television, Cardinal Jean Marie Lustiger, Archbishop of Paris, was interviewed by a journalist.

"Your Eminence," he asked, "do you believe in the existence of the devil?"

"Yes, I do."

"But in an era of such tremendous progress in the fields of science and technology, you still believe in the existence of the devil?"

"Yes, I still believe."

"Have you seen the devil?"

"Yes, I've seen him."

"Where?"

"At Dachau, at Auschwitz, at Birkenau!"

At this point, the journalist fell silent.

If someone should ask me, "Have you seen the Holy Spirit?" I too would respond without hesitation: "Yes, I've seen him."

"Where?"

"In the Church, but also outside the Church."

I have seen the Holy Spirit, "living Spring, living Fire, true Love," in the Popes of this century

In the twentieth century, the world has been torn apart by two world wars, ethnic conflicts, genocide, and bloody battles. Never before, in the history of the world, has there been such a slaughter of victims, not to mention all the evil done by ideological wars.... Within the Church there were real crises and defections; we again experienced a de-Christianization and secularization; the bark of Peter risked going down in the midst of the storm.

Still, perhaps the Church has never had such a sequence of Popes as great as those of the last century: Leo XIII, Pius X, Benedict XV, Pius XI, Pius XII, John XXIII, Paul VI, John Paul I, and John Paul II. I think that no country in the world during this same period has had the fortune to see a succession of responsible leaders at a similar level of morality, holiness, and competence.

We are before the action of the Holy Spirit who confirmed with his work the promise of Jesus: "You are Peter and on this rock I will build my Church and the gates of hell shall not prevail against it" (Mt 16:18).

The Holy Spirit has guided and continues to guide the ministry and the Magisterium of the Popes.

I have seen the Holy Spirit, "Lord and giver of life," in the history of the Church

We all know the work of the Holy Spirit in the first Christian centuries: the rapid spread of Christianity throughout the entire Roman Empire; the particular action of the Holy Spirit in the ecumenical councils that focused on trinitarian and christological doctrine; the powerful breath of the Holy Spirit in the birth of monasticism, which prevented Christians from becoming worldly and kept the yearning for holiness alive.

During the Middle Ages, when a new danger seemed to threaten the Church, the Spirit not only caused monasticism to flourish again, but also raised up new forms of consecrated life to respond better to the needs of the times. In a letter of the Roman Curia, written by order of Pope Alexander IV concerning St. Francis and St. Clare of Assisi, we read:

> The vision of faith has been clouded and conduct has become uncertain and vacillating, as if the aged world were oppressed by the weight of its years.... And behold, God, who loves humanity, from the secret of his mercy foresees and raises up in the Church new religious Orders, providing through them a support to the faith as well as a norm for reforming customs. I would not hesitate to call the new founders, with their true followers, light for the world, guides to show the way, teachers of life.[1]

What is said here could be said of all the great founders. It could be said of many inspired women like the three Doctors of the Church: Catherine of Siena, Teresa of Avila, and Therese of the Child Jesus. It could also be said of the two co-patrons of Europe in addition to Catherine: Bridget of Sweden and Edith Stein. In them is manifested the powerful action of the Holy Spirit.

Let us rest our gaze on the last decade of the Church's history, from the Second Vatican Council to the Jubilee of the year 2000. Are we not witnessing with astonishment a New Pentecost? Perhaps never before as today has there been such a flowering of holiness in typically lay activity. It is a true and new springtime of the Church. It is enough to think of the World Youth Days celebrated in Rome, Buenos Aires, Com-

---

1. *Fonti Francescane*, II, Assisi: 1997, pp. 2391–2393 *passim*.

postella, Czestochowa, Denver, Manila, Paris, and Rome. Young people all gathered around the Holy Father, desiring to hear the Word of God and committed to living it. We can think of the Convention of Church Movements and Ecclesial Communities on the vigil of Pentecost, May 30, 1998. New charisms are breaking forth in the Church, true gifts of the Spirit, and are making the Gospel flourish again in our world.

Observing that multitude of people animated by the Spirit in St. Peter's Square, the Holy Father could say: "What happened two thousand years ago in Jerusalem—it is as though this evening it is renewed in this Piazza, center of the Christian world. Like the Apostles, we too find ourselves gathered in a great Cenacle of Pentecost, yearning for the effusion of the Spirit."

He added later:

Whenever he intervenes, the Spirit always leaves us in wonder. He gives rise to events, the newness of which stupefies us; he radically changes persons and history. This was the unforgettable experience of the Second Vatican Council, during which, beneath the guidance of the same Spirit, the Church discovered her own charismatic dimension: "It is not only through the sacraments and the ministries of the Church that the Holy Spirit sanctifies and leads the People of God and enriches it with virtues, but, 'allotting his gifts to everyone according as he wills' (1 Cor 12:11), he distributes special graces among the faithful of every rank. By these gifts he makes them fit and ready to undertake the various tasks and offices which contribute toward the renewal and building up of the Church" (*Lumen Gentium,* n.12).[2]

---

2. *L'Osservatore Romano,* June 1–2, 1998, p. 6.

I have seen that without the Holy Spirit we can do nothing good: "If you take your grace away, nothing pure in man will stay"

It is true that after the first enthusiasm engendered by ι Second Vatican Council, there was a time of bewilderment. the face of the changes that the Spirit called for, some, trus ing too much in their own ideas and resources, took the wron course and created distress and sometimes discord. Instead o a yearned-for springtime, it seemed an unexpectedly icy win ter had arrived. "But it is here," as Cardinal Ratzinger said at the Convention of Ecclesial Movements, "that the Holy Spirit, so to speak, has again asked to have the floor. In young men and women the faith flowered again, without 'ifs' or 'buts,' without subterfuges or loopholes, lived in its wholeness as a gift, as a precious gift which gives life."[3]

Regarding the action of the Holy Spirit in the Church, the present Orthodox Patriarch of Antioch, Ignatius Hazim, said at Uppsala in 1968:

> Without the Holy Spirit, God is distant, Christ is in the past, the Gospel is a dead letter, the Church is a simple organization, authority is domination, mission is propaganda, worship is the summoning of spirits, and Christian action the morality of slaves.... But in him...the Risen Christ is here, the Gospel is the power of life, the Church means trinitarian communion, authority is a liberating service, mission is a Pentecost, liturgy is memorial and anticipation, human behavior is deified.[4]

---

3. J. Ratzinger, *I Movimenti Ecclesiali e la Loro Collocazione Teologia*, in: AA.VV., *I Movimenti nella Chiesa: Atti del Congresso Mondiale dei Movimenti Ecclesiali.* Rome: May 27–29, 1998, Libreria Editrice Vaticana, 1999, pp. 2–4.

4. I. Hazim, *La Risurrezione e L'Uomo di Oggi.* Rome: 1970, pp. 25–26.

In the Synod of Asian Bishops, the laity asked the bishops not to trust only in their organizational abilities, acting like good *managers,* but to be true *fathers*, shepherds, and credible witnesses to the love of God for humanity.

I very much like to recall what St. John Chrysostom wrote when he presented the Apostles as authentic examples of true shepherds:

> The Apostles did not come down from the mountain like Moses with stone tablets in their hands. They emerged from the Cenacle carrying the Holy Spirit in their hearts and offering everywhere treasures of wisdom and of grace as spiritual gifts flowing from a gushing spring. They went preaching to the whole world, they themselves being the living law, as if they were books animated by the grace of the Holy Spirit.[5]

I have seen the Holy Spirit working in a Church that always renews itself

The Church renews and purifies herself "led by the Holy Spirit" *(Gaudium et Spes,* n. 21).

For such a renewal, the Church of our day feels the need to return with fidelity to its sources: to Ur of Chaldea, to Sinai, to Jerusalem, Bethlehem, Nazareth, to the Mount of the Beatitudes, and to the Holy Sepulchre.

It is also necessary that the People of God make an examination of conscience.

The Church, by virtue of the Holy Spirit, is mother and virgin, and she remains the faithful spouse of the Lord—holy, without sin, but asking pardon for her sons and daughters who are sinners.

---

5. *In Mt. Hom.*, 1, 1: PG 57–58, 15.

We think in particular of the most important ecclesial event of the twentieth century. For a great renewal of the Church, the Holy Spirit inspired Pope John XXIII to plant a "small seed"[6] announcing on January 25, 1959, the convocation of the Second Vatican Council. He could not have imagined what this event would bring with it: the reforms of the Church, of the Roman Curia; the publication of the new *Code of Canon Law,* the *Code of Canons for the Oriental Churches,* the *Catechism of the Catholic Church,* so many important encyclical letters, the new Roman Missal; collegiality; ecumenical dialogue; interreligious dialogue; etc. The preparation and opening of the Great Jubilee of the year 2000 stimulates a deepening of this rich inheritance on the part of new generations.

It is possible to continue; we could cite other facts, other innovations quickened in the heart of the Church by the Holy Spirit. In reality, it is impossible to have a complete vision of the work of the Spirit in the twentieth century because it is also a mystery in the depths of souls.

It is enough to remember words of admiration from the world: "Twenty centuries were needed to be able to travel one kilometer from the Vatican to the Synagogue, and Pope Wojtyla has been the first to do it!"

Thank you, Holy Father!

I have also seen the Holy Spirit outside the Church

While he sustains and enlightens the Apostles, the Holy Spirit stirs up a thirst for living water (cf. Jn 4:10–15) in the heart of every person, culture, and religion, to search for Jesus, the only Savior who can fully satisfy their thirst.

---

6. Apostolic Constitution *Humanae Salutis*, Dec. 25, 1961.

Acts recounts in chapter 10 the vision of Cornelius, a Roman official and unbeliever, and then the vision of Peter and the voice that said to him:

> "Get up, Peter! Kill and eat!" But Peter said, "Certainly not, Lord! I have never eaten anything that is unclean or impure!" And the voice came to him a second time, "What God has made clean, you must not call profane" (Acts 10:13–15).
>
> …While Peter was still saying these things, the Holy Spirit came upon all who were listening to the word. The believers who were of the circumcision who had accompanied Peter were astounded, because the gift of the Holy Spirit had also been poured out upon the Gentiles—they could hear them speaking in tongues and glorifying God. Then Peter responded, "Can anyone withhold the water of baptism from these people, who have received the Holy Spirit the same as we have?" (Acts 10:44–47)

The Spirit precedes, accompanies, and follows all of our missions.

With the gift of tongues the Spirit prepared the great dialogue of love between God and humanity, between the Savior and the peoples of every continent, reinforcing their witness according to the promise of Jesus: "When the Holy Spirit comes upon you, you will receive power and you will be my witnesses in Jerusalem and in all Judea and Samaria, all the way to the ends of the earth" (Acts 1:8).

Even today, in the new Pentecost that we are living, the Spirit guides the Church in its mission of realizing an encounter between Jesus Christ and all peoples. I think this is the most profound meaning of the various dialogues that the Catholic Church has undertaken since the Council.

I come from that vast continent of Asia, and every day I see this work of the Spirit among the "gentiles." The observation that St. Thomas attributes to St. Ambrose is accurate: *"Every truth, from whomever it proceeds, is from the Holy Spirit."*[7] Perhaps not only every truth is from the Holy Spirit, but also every goodness, justice, beauty, depth of prayer, and splendor of wisdom. It consoles us to see how the Spirit is at work to reveal fully the mystery of Christ.

I have seen the Holy Spirit, "Father of the poor," who has not abandoned us as orphans

During my long stay in prison, deprived of every human resource, I was more profoundly convinced of the strength of the Holy Spirit as presented in the Acts of the Apostles. This strength is indispensable for the Church even today, so that it can overcome every kind of trial.

For this reason, since the year 1975 I have always asked my penitents to read attentively, as penance after confession, a chapter of the Acts of the Apostles.

Yes, the Holy Spirit lives and acts in the hearts of the poor and the humble, in popular piety, in solidarity, in suffering. He is there as an advocate and interpreter of desires and of prayer.

One day a pastor in North Vietnam watched as a group from the H'Mống peoples arrived in the town.

"Where are you from?" he asked them.

"We're from Lai Châu [where the battle of Điện Biên Phủ, which defeated the French, took place in 1954]. We have walked for six days on foot through the mountains."

"My Lord! For what?"

"We want to be baptized right away."

---

7. St. Thomas Aquinas, *Summa Theologiae* I–II, q. 109, a. 1, ad 1; the same thought in *De Veritate,* q. 1, a. 8. The text is probably from *Ambrosiaster: Comm. In 1 Cor* 12, 3: PL 17, 258: *"Quidquid enim verum a quocumque dicitur, a Sancto dicitur Spiritu."*

"That's impossible! There are no priests or catechists among you. You don't know the Faith or your prayers."

"We learned everything from a radio station in the Philippines."

"What radio station? There's no Catholic broadcast transmitted in your dialect!"

"It was the station, *Source of Life!*"

"A Protestant station! Now you are here to become Catholic? What a surprise!" Deeply moved, the pastor exclaimed, "A new Pentecost! The work of the Holy Spirit! The Holy Spirit!" And he asked them, "Can't you remain a few days longer?"

"Father, it's impossible. We've brought only enough rice with us for fourteen days: twelve days of travel and two days of study and prayer…."

They were baptized, therefore, and confirmed, and took part for the first time in Holy Mass and received the Eucharist.

"You won't have any more Masses, you don't even have a church. How will you manage?"

"In the evenings we listen to the radio in groups of three or four families in order to pray together and study the Faith. On Sundays, we work in the rice camps, but at 9:30 we stop work, let the buffaloes loose, and take part in Mass via *Radio Veritas* from Manila."

I would like to take this opportunity to profoundly thank *Radio Veritas* and *Radio Vaticana,* which carry out this precious work of evangelization through the Vietnamese and H'Mống programs. Now, the H'Mống are happy to have a broadcast in their own language.

In the meantime, those first baptized brought their faith to another 5,000 fellow citizens. The Holy Spirit has not left them orphans.

Come, Holy Spirit

Paul VI spoke in a splendid manner of the Holy Spirit as the soul of the Church:

The Holy Spirit is the animator and sanctifier of the Church, her divine breath, the wind in her sails, her unifying principle, her interior source of light and strength, her support and her consoler, her source of charisms and songs, her peace and her joy, her reward and prelude of blessed and eternal life. The Church needs this perennial Pentecost; it needs fire in the heart, words on her lips, prophecy in her glance.[8]

For this, we also trustingly invoke, *"Come, Holy Spirit."*

Edith Stein, co-patron of Europe, prayed this prayer on the last Pentecost of her life:

Who are you, sweet light, who fills me
and brightens the darkness of my heart?
You guide me like a maternal hand,
and if you were to abandon me
I could not take another step.
You are the space which encircles
my being and encloses me within itself.
If you were to leave me,
I would fall into the abyss of nothingness,
from which you elevate me into Light.
You are closer to me than I am to myself,
and more intimate than my innermost being,
and everywhere elusive and incomprehensible,
beyond every name: Holy Spirit, eternal Love.[9]

---

8. Words pronounced at the General Audience of Wednesday, Nov. 29, 1972: *Teachings of Paul VI,* X (1972), Città del Vaticano: 1973, pp. 1210–1211.

9. *Werke*, XI, Druten/Freiburg-Basel-Wien, 1987, p. 175.

20
BEHOLD YOUR MOTHER
The Model of the Church

"The joy of the Jubilee would not be complete if our gaze did not turn to the one who, in full obedience to the Father, gave birth to the Son of God in the flesh for our sake."[1]

The Virgin at midday

In these days, I have had the privilege of being in silence to contemplate the Blessed Virgin Mary, so well represented in this chapel of the *Mother of the Redeemer.* Then from my heart rose this prayer by Paul Claudel († 1955).

> It is midday. I see the Church open. I need to go in.
> Mother of Jesus Christ, I have not come to pray.

> I have nothing to offer you or ask of you.
> I come only, O Mother, to look at you.
> To look at you, to cry for joy....

> Without saying anything, to gaze on your face,
> to allow the heart to sing its own language.
> Not to say anything, but only to sing,
> because the heart is too full.[2]

---

1. John Paul II, Bull of Indiction of the Great Jubilee, *Incarnationis Mysterium.* Boston: Pauline Books & Media, 1999, n. 14.

2. *Oeuvre Poétique.* Paris: Éditions Gallimard, 1967, pp. 539 ff.

The Church is a Woman, a Mother

Some words of Cardinal Joseph Ratzinger have given me inspiration for this meditation:

> The Church is not an apparatus; she is not simply an institution; neither is she only one of the usual sociological entities—she is a person. She is a Woman. She is a Mother. She is alive. The Marian understanding of the Church is the strongest and most decisive contrast with the concept of a purely organizational and bureaucratic Church. We cannot make the Church; we must *be* the Church. It is only in the measure in which faith, above and beyond doing, forms our being, that we *are* Church and the Church is in us. And it is only in being Marian that we become Church. Also at the beginning, the Church was not made, but born. She was born when the *fiat* emerged from the soul of Mary. This is the most profound desire of the Council: that the Church is reawakened in our souls. Mary shows us the way.[3]

In this meditation, we want to look at Mary as the model of the Church. The Church lives in a sad, dramatic, and magnificent land, in an age that has the traits of a "collective dark night."[4]

Among the characteristics of this night there is the prevalence of rationalism, which has molded a culture that tends, through the various sciences, to manipulate natural realities, situations, and even the spirit and human life. Thus, humanity risks becoming the victim of the mere positivism of "doing" and "having."

The Church's response to this night is to be love, because, as the title of a small book by Hans Urs von Balthasar affirms,

---

3. J. Ratzinger, *Die Ekklesiologie des Zweiten Vatikanums,* in: IKZt 15 (1986), p. 52.

4. Cf. Teachings of John Paul II, V/3 (1982). Cittá del Vaticano: 1983, pp. 1141–1142.

"Only love is credible." Without love to the point of unity, there is no credibility.

For this reason, Mary "shows us the way." She is:

Love welcomed,

Love reciprocated,

Love shared.

Mary is love welcomed

During the entire span of her life, Mary received everything from God. Precisely in this lies the greatness of her mission, which is mysteriously prolonged in the Church. Everything comes from the Lord, arrives from on high, and the Virgin welcomes it.

Let us reflect, together with the whole Church, on four phrases of Scripture.

1. Hail Mary, full of grace.

From the beginning, Mary receives the Good News, and from the beginning, in expectation of the passion of Jesus, she is filled with the fullness of salvation. With the angel's greeting, the handmaiden becomes *possessed by God*. We are at the dawn of a Church that is, as *Lumen Gentium* states, "the field or tillage of God" (n. 6; cf. 1 Cor 3:9).

2. Behold, you will conceive and bear a son.

Through the work of the Holy Spirit, the great mystery of the Incarnation is realized. The Son, who in heaven lived *in the bosom of the Father,* on earth finds in Mary a womb worthy of himself. Daughter of the Father, Mary becomes mother—Mother of the Word Incarnate, Spouse of the Holy Spirit. In the nine months that follow the Angel's greeting, Mary is especially the Virgin of interiority. Unique among creatures, she has the experience of *carrying Jesus physically in her womb.* Reflecting her, the whole Church is called to be a "womb" that offers Jesus to the world.

3. He has looked upon my lowliness.

Throughout her life, Mary lived a song of gratitude to God for what she received from him—not only grace, but the Giver of grace, and with him all other privileges. "For the Mighty One has done great things for me...he has looked with favor on the lowliness of his servant." Because of this, "all generations will call me blessed." Like Mary, the Church, aware of her *nothingness,* proclaims the greatness of the Lord.

4. She treasured all these words in her heart.

In total recollection, Mary lives alongside her Son "in the state" of prayer, of perennial acceptance, and of contemplation. She guards the Word, lives and communicates it in hope, in humility, and in joy. Let us contemplate in her—she who is completely animated *by the Word*—the mystery of the Church, the *Spouse of the Word.*

Mary, you are all beautiful and in you there is no blemish. From you was born Christ our God.

Mary is love reciprocated

Filled with the grace of God, Mary responded to God with her whole being. There was nothing in her that was not a self-giving gift, an acceptance of God's plans, and a choice of God.

Here, too, let us reflect on some words of Scripture that speak about Mary.

5. Blessed is she who believed.

In faith, Mary lived a total "yes," because she believed in the Word. She let herself be shaped by the hand of God and led everywhere by him: to Egypt, Nazareth, Cana, Golgotha, and to the Cenacle in expectation of the Spirit. Elizabeth and the early community spoke of her as, *"she who believed."* In her, the Church sees itself as the *community of believers.*

6. *He was subject to them.*

For 33 years, Mary was in tender, intimate communion with Jesus. No other human being can understand Jesus as much as Mary; no one is as close to him, for no one took daily care of him as did Mary: in work, in joy, in anxiety, in poverty, in pain. For us, this is a call to *intimacy* with Jesus, to a concrete and attentive *service* in his regard.

7. *My soul glorifies the Lord.*

Aware of the marvels that God has accomplished in her, Mary is in contemplative adoration before God, like the angels who proclaim: "holy, holy, holy." Thus, Mary is a full response to the mercy of God, which he extends "from generation to generation."

For us, this is an invitation to constant *praise* and *adoration.*

8. *By the cross of Jesus stood his mother.*

As throughout her entire life, Mary is also united to Jesus in his passion and death for humanity. A sword pierces her heart. She remains standing alone and courageous. She knows how to forgive and she remains faithful. At the most important moment in the life of Jesus, she offers herself together with him. For Mary all seems lost, but it is enough to *be with Jesus.* She is the prototype of the Church beneath the cross.

Here I would like to add an incident from my own life.

When I studied at Rome in 1957, I went to Lourdes to pray to the Blessed Mother. Finding myself at the grotto, I meditated on the words of Mary to St. Bernadette: "I do not promise you joy and consolations on this earth, but trials and sufferings." I had the deep impression that these words were also addressed to me. I accepted this message, though not without some fear.

Returning to Vietnam, I became a professor, then the rector of the seminary, the vicar general, and finally bishop of Nha Trang. One could say that my pastoral ministry was crowned with success. Every year, I returned to Lourdes and often wondered to myself, "Perhaps the words addressed to Bernadette are not for me." The year 1975 arrived and with it my arrest on the Feast of the Assumption, my imprisonment, my isolation. Then I understood that the Blessed Mother had been preparing me for this since 1957!

Mary is love shared

Being all of God, Mary is no stranger to the world. Rather, for her the world is the place where God encounters humanity, where one waits for him who, "for us men and for our salvation came down from heaven."

Together with the whole Church, let us reflect on Mary who is the "land of the One who cannot be contained," the one who welcomed salvation and *shared* it.

9. She went with haste into the hill country.

Mary brings the good news which is Jesus immediately to her cousin Elizabeth. She shares the love that God has communicated to her; she remains for six months at the service of her cousin; she causes John the Baptist to leap at the nearness of salvation. She continues to live with Jesus in her womb, feeling God made man growing within her. This is the way of the Church: *to serve humanity,* bringing and communicating Jesus who lives in us, and thus, bringing salvation and joy. Who knows how many times Elizabeth and Mary sang the *Magnificat* together!

10. They found the child with Mary his mother.

Mary is the messenger of mercy. In the extreme poverty of the crib, she brings the world the greatest treasure. It is the manifestation of Jesus. Mary shows him and offers him to the shepherds and to the magi, to the first fruits of Israel, and to the gentiles. She continues to do so even today—at Guadalupe as in my own country at Lavang. Mary shows Jesus to the poor, to the stranger. She is the star of *evangelization,* and she shows us the way of mission.

11. Do whatever he tells you.

With Jesus, Mary is present for all the normal realities of life. She is present at Ain Karim for the birth of Elizabeth's son, and at Cana for a wedding feast. She shares joy and hope. She exerts herself with delicacy, gentleness, and discretion for the young married couple in distress. She teaches them to listen to Jesus and to trust that he will help when the moment comes. She shares with the Apostles the expectation of the Spirit in the Cenacle. Living in the midst of everyone, in everyday life, Mary is the model of *a Church who knows how to await and welcome the hour of God:* the descent of the Holy Spirit.

12. "There is your son"…and the disciple took her into his care.

Near the cross, Mary accepts all of the disciples of Jesus as her children, indeed all of humanity—not only the saints, but also the sinners. She offers her son Jesus, the Most Holy, and accepts John, the fearful disciple who fled Gethsemane. She accepts the good thief, the criminal who became a saint and a brother of Jesus who promised: "Amen, I say to you, this day you will be with me in Paradise" (Lk 23:43). At that moment, Mary accepts her role as *Mother of Mercy.* Then she spends her life with the apostle John, the beloved, sharing her concern for the Kingdom. From her John learns always anew what he learned from Jesus: God is Love, and we are called only to be love. As the Mother of Mercy, Mary urges the Church *to carry the burdens of all humanity* in its fundamental needs, not only through the good example of Christians, but also by means of their undertakings on the social, economic, and political levels.

Mystery—communion—mission

With Mary, who we invoke in the *Salve Regina* as *"our hope,"* the future of the Church is full of hope.

Profoundly devoted to the Mother of the Lord, the Holy Father said: "At the dawn of the new millennium we perceive with joy the emergence of that 'Marian profile' of the Church, which contains within itself the most profound content of the conciliar renewal."[5]

From Mary the Church learns to fulfill with exactness that profile which the Second Vatican Council modeled on her:

- to live immersed in the *Mystery:* love welcomed;
- to form *communion* in all the aspects of its life: love reciprocated;
- to project oneself toward the world in *mission:* love shared.

Following the Mother of Jesus, the Church runs along the way of Mary, as John Paul II explained in his encyclical, *Mother of the Redeemer.*

The twelve phrases from the Gospel, in which we have contemplated the icon of Mary, accompany us on this journey. They are like the twelve stars that adorn the crown of the Virgin and which the Book of Revelation speaks of in the liturgy of the Assumption.

---

5. John Paul II in a catechesis on the signs of hope present in the Church, in: *L'Osservatore Romano*, Nov. 26, 1998, p. 6.

Mary sets me free

During the journey into the obscurity of being a prisoner, I prayed to Mary with all simplicity, "Mother, if you see that I can no longer be useful to your Church, grant me the grace to consume my life in prison. Otherwise, allow me to leave prison on one of your feasts."

Then, one day while I was preparing lunch, I heard the guard's telephone ringing. "Perhaps this phone call is for me!" I thought. "Today is November 21, the Feast of the Presentation of Mary in the Temple!" Soon afterward, one of the guards came to me and asked:

"Did you finish lunch?"

"Not yet!"

"After lunch, make yourself presentable. You're going to see the chief."

That afternoon I met the Minister of the Interior.

"Do you have a desire to express?"

"Yes, sir. I want my freedom."

"When?"

"Today."

Usually it's impossible to ask for "today," because the leaders need time to discuss the formalities of release. But I had a lot of faith.

The Minister looked at me very surprised. I explained:

"Sir, I have been in prison for too long—under three pontificates: those of Paul VI, John Paul I, and John Paul II; and besides that, under *four* Secretary Generals of the Soviet Communist Party: Brezhnev, Andropov, Chernenko, and Gorbachev!"

He began to laugh and nodded his head.

"It's true, it's true!"

Then, turning toward his secretary he said, "Do whatever is necessary to fulfill his request."

I rejoiced! Mary had freed me. Thanks be to you, dear Mother! Happy Feast Day!

Hail Mary, Mother of Jesus,
Mother and model of his Church.
Hail, font of grace and of mercy,
model of all purity.
Hail, joy in tears,
victory in battles,
hope in trials,
the only way to Jesus.

Show us the Father and that will be enough for us. Show yourself a mother and that will be enough for us.

21
Now and at the Hour of Our Death
Old Age, Infirmity, Death

In the Asian Buddhist culture one speaks of four stages of human life: birth, old age, infirmity, and death. In each of these stages there is suffering; this is the inevitable human destiny, which pleads for salvation.

Usually people do not like to recall these realities. One almost wishes to remove them from one's life and not have to think of them. However, for the Christian whose vocation it is to love, these too are love. Like every other moment of life, whether painful or joyful, they are to be lived in love and as love.

When I see the crowds of Jubilee pilgrims walking toward the Holy Door, I think about life. We go forward every day on ways that are sometimes difficult yet important and not without joy, because we are coming closer to the goal, to the encounter with Jesus, our hope.

For this reason, I would like to speak of old age, infirmity, and death.

The greatest gift

"You show me the path of life. In your presence there is fullness of joy" (Ps 16:11).

Life is the greatest good God has given to human beings. It is priceless. Every instant of our life is lived in him and through him.

For each of us life has its seasons, and each season is important and beautiful with a beauty all its own. Cicero speaks of old age as the "autumn of life."[1] Pope John Paul II, the poet, paints a lovely picture:

> We need but to look at the changes taking place in the landscape over the course of the year, on the mountains and in the plains, in the meadows, valleys and forests, in the trees and plants. There is a close resemblance between our human biorhythms and the natural cycles of which we are a part.[2]

Yes, for the life that is born, the life that grows, and the life that declines are merely three moments in the mystery of existence, in that human life which comes from God. It is his gift, his image, his imprint, and a participation in his life-giving breath.[3]

The elderly in Sacred Scripture

In Sacred Scripture, longevity is a sign of the favor and the love of God (cf. Gen 11:10–32). Abraham, Moses, Tobit, Eleazar, Elizabeth and Zechariah, Simeon and Anna show us how old age can be a time of promise and courageous witness.

In old age, Peter gave his life for love of Jesus.

Aged and in prison, Paul wrote: "My life is already being poured out like a libation…. I have finished the race, I have kept the faith" (2 Tim 4:6–7).

---

1. Cf. Cicero, *Cato Maior, seu de Senectute* 19, 70.
2. John Paul II, *To the Elderly*. Boston: Pauline Books & Media, 1999, n. 5.
3. Cf. John Paul II, in: *L'Osservatore Romano,* Nov. 1, 1998.

When already quite old, St. John the Apostle visited the Christian communities. Whenever he was asked what Jesus' message was, he always repeated: "Love one another," as if he could add nothing else. Yet, with this phrase, he truly penetrates the heart of Christ's thought.

A new, more charismatic assignment

In the course of my life, and particularly here in the Roman Curia, I have been privileged to know many elderly people, men and women who have profoundly edified me with their humble and discreet but eloquent example. They remain young always, and whoever comes near them breathes an air of comfort and of hope even in almost desperate situations.

From them I have learned that the years go by quickly, that the gift of life is very beautiful and precious, and that I must make the most of the present moment with gratitude to the *Father of mercies* (cf. Col 5:16). I have also learned that I must know how and when to retire. Not so I can watch my strength decline, or to feel the always more impending threat of solitude, or to risk feeling myself useless, marginalized, a weight on others. Rather, in order to carry out a new assignment that is more suitable, more committed, and more charismatic. Our ability to work diminishes, but our love always grows. Radiantly, one draws near to the hope of which Paul speaks: "there is reserved for me the crown of righteousness" (2 Tim 4:8).

The Holy Father, John Paul II, has left us words of great comfort and hope:

> My thoughts turn...to you, dear brother priests and bishops, who, for reasons of age, no longer have direct responsibility for pastoral ministry. The Church still needs you. She appreciates the services which you may wish to provide in many areas of the apostolate; she

counts on the support of your longer periods of prayer; she counts on your advice born of experience, and she is enriched by your daily witness to the Gospel.[4]

Giuse Maria Trịnh Như Khuí, the first Cardinal of Vietnam and Archbishop of Hanoi, was not permitted by the government to go to the parishes for confirmations and to make pastoral visits. Every morning for twenty years he went to the terrace of his home and prayed the rosary for his faithful. Ten years after his death and just after my release from prison, I went to his home. I was profoundly moved when I saw, in an oval shape, the tracks his pacing had worn onto the floor of this terrace—signs of the faith of an old pastor. I thought of what Pope John XXIII wrote to a bishop, "Now your work has changed [regarding the Church], you have to pray for her. And that is no less important than action."

Infirmity

"The days of our life are seventy years, or perhaps eighty, if we are strong, even then their span is only toil and trouble; they are soon gone, and we fly away" (Ps 90:10).

Aside from what we can consider the "natural illness" of old age, there are also infirmities, which can strike at any age.

In this, I also have had some experience. During my imprisonment, I underwent surgery five times. Twice I was close to death because of serious infections. I received the anointing of the sick, which was administered by five of my brother bishops who wept because they were moved with compassion by my desperate situation.

---

4. John Paul II, *To the Elderly*. Boston: Pauline Books & Media, 1999, n. 13.

To understand what place illness occupies in the divine plan, we have to focus on the value of the human body.

Paul VI affirms that:

> The human body is sacred.... Yes, the divine lives there.... And more, when grace sanctifies man, his body is not only an instrument of the soul, it is also the mysterious temple of the Holy Spirit.... A new concept of human flesh opens before our eyes...which does not alter the vision of physical and biological reality.... It is filled with a new attraction, which neither pleasure nor beauty suggests, but which the love of Christ inspires.[5]

Valuing physical and moral trials

Christian love gives value and meaning to our existence even when infirmity and illness have compromised the integrity of the body. There is a life in us not conditioned by our physical state, but by the love we give. "You who are sick, you are strong like Jesus on the cross," exclaimed John Paul II one day. Yes, because our strength is in Christ, in Christ crucified and abandoned! It is when we are weak that we are strong.

I touched this reality in prison. When I lived through times of extreme physical and moral suffering, I thought of Jesus crucified. To the human eye, his life was a defeat, a disappointment, and a failure. Reduced to the most absolute immobility on the cross, he was no longer able to encounter people, to cure the sick, to teach.... However, in the eyes of God, that was the most important moment of his life, because it was then that he poured out his blood for the salvation of humanity.

---

5. *Teachings of Paul VI*, I (1963). Cittá del Vaticano: 1965, p. 141.

"Everyone is invited to cross this threshold," John Paul II said at the Jubilee of the Sick, to cross the threshold of the Door of life, the Door of salvation that is Jesus. John Paul II recalled how pain and sickness are a part of the mystery of humanity on earth. "The 'key' to this reading [of the design of God] is found in the *Cross of Christ....* One who knows how to accept it in his own life, experiences how pain, illumined by faith, becomes a source of hope and of salvation."[6]

Death

"With humble and serene faith" (Paul VI).

The serene thought of death accompanied Pope John XXIII throughout his life. The first draft of his spiritual testament dates from 1925, the year of his episcopal ordination and thirty-eight years before his death.

The testament of Paul VI consists of a document dated June 30, 1965, thirteen years before his death.

These two great Popes have given us an example of the faith that fixes "its gaze on the mystery of death and of what follows it, in the light of Christ who alone gives it light."[7]

There are two pivotal moments in everyone's life: birth and death. The earthly life we begin and the life we complete by crossing the threshold of time toward eternity. This final moment is always accompanied by strong and particularly intense human sentiments.

Death is the most serious matter in life. Among all of life's trials, it is the greatest. It is definitive. Death is the culmination of our life, the last offering that we can give to

---

6. "Homily for the Jubilee of the Sick," in: *L'Ossertavore Romano*, Feb. 12, 2000.

7. Testament of Paul VI, n. 1 in: *L'Osservatore Romano,* Aug. 12, 1978.

God here on earth. But we can be sure that in that hour we will be assisted, like Joseph, by Jesus and Mary.

The Christian vision of death's hour is well expressed in one of the prefaces for the Mass for the Dead: "For your faithful, life is not taken away, but transformed; and while our earthly dwelling is destroyed, an eternal home will be prepared in heaven."

There is a Vietnamese saying, "Birth is a pilgrimage, death a return home." For this reason, the deceased are buried facing the mountains in my country, as if, like Jesus at the Ascension, they will go up to heaven from those peaks.

To live for that hour

Jesus' life culminated with the Paschal Mystery. He has shown us the road to reach Heaven: he first walked the way to Calvary. He chose no other way to end his earthly work.

He came to earth, healed the sick, preached the Good News, and founded the Church, but above all he lived for his "hour." He lived for the hour when he would be lifted on the cross and draw everyone to himself (cf. Jn 12:32). In that "hour" he accomplished his work.

Like Jesus, we must live for our own "hour." Each of us has an "hour," and it is good to live in expectation of it and to offer it now for the purposes God has entrusted to us, even if we are in the full vigor of physical strength.

This is the most "beautiful hour," the "hour" of life and not so much of death. That hour is the moment of our encounter with Jesus—we will see him! It is there that he waits for us, and with him, we will meet Mary, who we have so often called upon in life to intercede for us "now and at the hour of our death." As a loving Mother, Mary will welcome and lead us to the Father as her favored children.

The examination of mercy

In the second meditation, I presented five defects of Jesus. Now I will add a sixth. As a teacher, Jesus would certainly be dismissed by the Department of Education for already revealing the content of the final exam that should be kept secret. More than that, he describes the unfolding of the exam. "But when the son of man comes in his glory…all the nations will be gathered before him, and he will separate them from each other, the way a shepherd separates the sheep from the goats" (cf. Mt 25:31–33). The theme of that judgment will be love: "Amen, I say to you, insofar as you did it for one of these least of my brothers, you did it for me" (Mt 25:40).

And Jesus is not only guilty of having revealed the content of the exam, he has also simplified it, substituting the ten demands of the Decalogue with a summary: "Love God and your neighbor."

Jesus, you are our teacher, our judge, our reward! I have no more fear of being judged, but I ardently desire to meet my judge who is so good, generous, and merciful.

Jesus, our only joy be you,
as you our prize will be;
Jesus, be you our glory true
throughout eternity.[8]

The supreme act of love

I would like to conclude this meditation with two testimonies.

I remember an account of the last moments of the life of Fr. Joseph Lagrange, O.P., founder of the Biblical School at Jerusalem and an example of courage, humility, and faith

---

8. The hymn, *Iesu dulcis memoria.*

under trial. He had been in a coma for a long time when, in the presence of his confreres, he suddenly sat up in bed, opened his eyes and, with his hands extended upward, exclaimed: "Jerusalem, Jerusalem!" It seemed as if he had seen the heavenly Jerusalem. Then he slowly closed his eyes, inclined his head, and breathed his last.

And in his testament, Paul VI wrote:

> In the face of death, the complete and definitive detachment from the present life, I feel the duty of celebrating the gift, the fortune, the beauty, the destiny of this fleeting existence. Lord, I thank you for having called me to life, and still more, that in making me a Christian, you have regenerated and destined me for the fullness of life.... I feel that the Church encircles me: holy Church, one and catholic and apostolic, receive with my blessed greetings, my supreme act of love (n. 1).[9]

---

9. Testament of Paul VI, n. 1 in: *L'Osservatore Romano,* Aug. 12, 1978.

22

THE CLOTHES OF MOURNING WILL BE TURNED INTO JOY

The Joy of Hope

Amid tall cypresses and blooming fig trees, with the perfume of the first flowers of spring, the sun is beginning to set. The air is fresh. Two men hurry along on their way to Emmaus, a village some 11 kilometers from Jerusalem. They are dejected (cf. Lk 24:13–35). Their sentiments, their vicissitudes, cause us to consider our own journey in this historic epoch of the Church.

On the road to Emmaus

The two disciples were sad and said, "We were hoping that he would be the one to liberate the people of Israel! But…." Likewise, humanly speaking, the Church sometimes feels tired, sad, and disappointed by the situation of today's world described in the fourth meditation. This is the disappointment of a Church that has placed its hopes on that which cannot return.

Jesus, whom the disciples take for a pilgrim, explains the Scriptures—beginning from Moses and proceeding with the prophets—to make them understand an enigmatic truth, "Was it not necessary that the Messiah should suffer these things and then enter into his glory?"

Christ, the Crucified Risen One, through his manifestation to the disciples at Emmaus, clearly reveals to us how the mystery of death and life, the cross and resurrection, are the keys to understanding the Scriptures and, with them, the life of the Church. Our hope is not consistent if it is not founded on the Word of God, on the mystery of the cross, and of the glorious Easter of Christ.

Christ is present in the Church when we read the Scriptures. His companionship with the disciples, the walk on the road with them, indicate the ineffable certainty of his being with us along the road of history as light that illumines the way and fire that burns in hearts.

At that moment of the "breaking of the bread"—a gesture that certainly reawakens the awareness of the two disciples—their eyes are opened and they recognize Jesus. Only with the eyes of faith can the Church recognize Jesus.

Jesus offers the disciples the Eucharistic bread and with it, enters their hearts. Not only is he there *with* them, in their midst, now he is also *within* them—a loving presence capable of changing their lives.

On the road to Emmaus, the disciples indicate the way to us. With the Eucharist, with the Word of God and the mystery of the cross, the Church can go forward humbly and with joy on its journey, sustained always by the presence of the Savior.

Reversal of course

"They got up," writes Luke, "and returned immediately to Jerusalem."

The power of Christ's presence worked a miracle. The disciples returned the way they had come. They returned to Jerusalem with hearts full of joy. Now they were witnesses, communicators of what they had experienced: the presence of Jesus in their midst, the overwhelming power of his Word that illumines all of Scripture, the friendship of the Risen One which inspired the cry, "Stay with us, because it is already evening!" Then, that meal offered by Jesus when, as the Risen One, he again gave himself to the disciples as the bread of resurrection and of life.

In Jerusalem, the two disciples found the eleven gathered together with their companions. They also knew that the Lord was risen from the dead. One to another, in the joy of their shared experience, they were, in a sense, re-evangelized by the announcement of the resurrection. Those of the Cenacle said, "The Lord has really risen and has been seen by Simon." The two from Emmaus confirmed this, reporting all that had happened to them along the way and how they had recognized him in the breaking of the bread (cf. Lk 24:33–35).

"Peace be with you"

Every time Jesus appears after the resurrection, his greeting is, "Peace be with you," or in other words, "I am with you." Jesus is our peace, our hope. For this reason the disciples of Emmaus acknowledge, "Were not our hearts burning within us while he spoke to us on the road, as he opened up the scriptures to us?" (Lk 24:32).

This true peace, which is the joy that the world cannot give, is achieved only on the road of a penitential journey, with a real change of life, as is asked of us in the Jubilee.

We must listen again to what the Spirit says to the seven churches which we contemplated in our third meditation, "Balancing Accounts at the Beginning of the Twenty-first Century." It is necessary always to emerge anew from the situation of a Church that has lost its first love, that tolerates idolatry, that yields to compromise—from the torpor of a Church that sleeps or lives half-heartedly, in mediocrity—to be a *poor Church, a Church that listens to the Holy Spirit, a Church of communion.*

To transform the human into the divine—this requires a *metanoia,* a radical change. A change like the gradual, then decisive change of the disciples of Emmaus who, converted by the Word and by the living presence of Christ, altered their direction. They had been fleeing from Jerusalem, city of the scandalous death of their Teacher in whom they had placed all their hopes. Now, without fear, they return to Jerusalem, city of the death and resurrection of their Lord.

A joy that no one can take away

With this attitude of purification, of a return to Christ, our sadness becomes joy.

Jesus had promised and now it is fulfilled: "Your grief will turn to joy...but I will see you again, and your hearts will rejoice, and no one will take your joy from you" (Jn 16:20–23). He is truly the faithful friend. The disciples saw him again and they experienced the joy of a presence that no one would ever take away from them.

No one else can give us this joy, which surpasses every possibility and all human understanding. On earth, we tend to someone who is sick as long as there is life. But who would tend to a corpse? That would be crazy! Jesus died, was buried, and is risen! From this is born our joy! An immense joy, always new, everlasting, because it is divine. *"O Beauty ever ancient, ever new, late have I loved you!"*[1]

In contemporary history, there is no lack of situations in which the Church lives "hoping against all hope": Situations of the suffering of feeling herself abandoned by the Father, of the suffering that comes from divisions among Christians, of the suffering of martyrdom, and of being a minority. It is precisely to this Church that the promise of Revelation re-

---

1. St. Augustine, *Confessions*, X, 27.

turns: "Death shall be no more—no more grief or crying or pain, for what came before has passed away" (21:4). There will be "a new heaven and a new earth" (cf. Rev 21:1).

If we began the spiritual exercises with the itinerary of the patriarchs in the book of Genesis, now we have opening before us Revelation's vision of peace.

Christ is in our midst through love

The peace that Jesus announces to his disciples is realized through love, the synthesis-commandment in which Jesus summed up the Decalogue of the Law of Moses: love for God and for one's neighbor. In love, the heart reconciles itself, reunites itself, and reacquires that peace for which we were created and for which we are destined.

On January 18, 2000, during the liturgy for the opening of the Holy Door at the Basilica of St. Paul outside the Walls, we had an almost prophetic experience of ecumenical peace expressed by an embrace of peace as a sign of mutual charity. Resounding within us still are the words of the Byzantine Liturgy recited on that occasion. "Let us love one another, so that in unity of spirit we may profess our faith in the Father, in the Son, and in the Holy Spirit." Then followed the words of the ancient Gregorian hymn taken from the Roman liturgy of Holy Thursday:

Where charity and love prevail
there God is ever found;
brought here together by Christ's love,
by love are we thus bound.

With grateful joy and holy fear
his charity we learn;
let us with heart and mind and soul
now love him in return.

Let strife among us be unknown,
let all contention cease;
be his the glory that we seek,
be ours his holy peace.

Let us recall that in our midst
dwells God's begotten Son;
As members of his body joined
we are in him made one.

Christ is in our midst as our peace and reconciliation, when we love God and when we love each other.

To be witnesses of hope

The episode of Emmaus reminds us all of a joyous reality of the Christian experience: the never-ending presence of the Risen Christ in the Church. It is a living and real presence, in the Word, in the sacraments, in the Eucharist. This presence also exists in and among persons, in the ministry of the Church, in the poor, in every brother and sister.

Celebrating the Great Jubilee, as the Holy Father has reminded us, we can say that our Jubilee *is* Christ, but he is also our jubilation, our joy! For 2000 years, the Church has lived of his presence. Looking toward the future, it has the unfailing hope of his promise: "I am with you always, to the end of the age" (Mt 28:20).

We have to be witnesses of this presence and of this hope. How can we truly be credible witnesses of this joy?

In these days together, we have lived a little of the walk to Emmaus. Now, to conclude the retreat and to leave a remembrance, as is customary, in a few key words I will summarize our commitment. Or, rather, our reciprocal agreement to live for each other, around the successor of Peter, as joyous witnesses of hope.

Let us learn from the disciples of Emmaus, by examining their reactions.

Let us return to Jerusalem

We return to the origins of the Gospel, and continually return to Jerusalem, as did the Holy Father in the Jubilee Year 2000. This is a return to the sources, to the center of the Church, a return to where Jesus was born, taught, suffered his passion, died, and was buried.

That seemed to be the end. Pilate sent his soldiers to guard the tomb of Jesus; the Jews rolled a huge stone in front of the sepulchre and put a seal on it. They wanted to destroy him forever, to erase him from everyone's memory, including his own disciples'.

Nevertheless, it was in Jerusalem that Jesus rose again and appeared to many people. The Church exults in joy because Jesus said: "Take courage; I have conquered the world" (Jn 16:33).

With the disciples of Emmaus we return to the authentic spirit of the Gospel, we return to the Paschal Mystery, the source of our hope!

Let us remain united
to the ecclesial community around Peter

In the Cenacle, the disciples of Emmaus found the Church community and Peter, the disciple to whom Jesus had promised to entrust his Church. To Peter was granted a special appearance of the Lord: "He has appeared to Simon" (cf. Lk 24:34).

Peter has an essential role of unity in the Church. For this reason, to Peter and to his successors God has given a particular grace of *martyria* (martyrdom), of testimony of faith in Jesus. Peter confesses his faith in Christ, the Son of the living

God. He runs to the sepulchre and discovers that the Lord is indeed risen. Standing before Jesus and the other disciples, he professes his love for the Master. On Vatican Hill in Rome, he seals his confession of faith and the primacy of charity with his blood.

The petrine profile of the Church is also the unity of faith and love for Christ around Peter, because the Church is one in her essence of love and service.

With Mary the Mother of Jesus

Although the Gospels do not say it, the intuition of the People of God confirms that the community of disciples, deprived of the physical presence of the Master before and especially after the Ascension, find in Mary, the Mother of Jesus, a guarantee of the Lord's continual assistance and an assurance of the promise of the Holy Spirit.

Mary, the Mother, spontaneously directs us to her Son. Mary, full of grace, full of the Holy Spirit, is the guarantee of the future outpouring of the Holy Spirit.

The Mother of Jesus—of the All-Holy—reveals the Marian profile of the Church, a family Church, a fraternal Church that is welcoming and solidly united. With Mary, we feel as brothers and sisters among ourselves, united in our confession of Christ. With Mary's merciful heart, we feel open to all people. Thus, the Church is catholic with the dimension of the Mother of unity who embraces all of her children dispersed throughout the world.

Mary, who is love *welcomed, reciprocated, and shared*, is the model of the Church which is Mystery, Communion, and Mission.

I believe in one, holy, catholic, apostolic, and joyous Church

We began these spiritual exercises with the Book of Genealogy, reflecting on Abraham's call, and we conclude with Abraham. Our hope is Jesus, the only Savior, who awaits us in the eternal joy of the banquet where the poor Lazarus also rests in the bosom of Abraham. Day after day, let us advance on our journey, sowing the seeds of hope for a new springtime in the Church—one, holy, catholic, apostolic, and *joyous.*

Jesus has already come into the world: "And the Word became flesh and lived among us" (Jn 1:14). "I am bringing you good news of great joy: Christ is born" (cf. Lk 2:10–11). The end times have already begun, even if inchoate, and will be complete only in Heaven.

During this earthly life, we already possess the joy of hope, because God has not only promised salvation "to our fathers, to Abraham and to his descendents for ever," but has also "sworn to Abraham, our Father…" (Lk 1:55–73). Our joy is so great and so inexpressible because it is guaranteed by God himself.

If a pilgrim arrives in Rome and obtains a ticket for an audience with the Pope from the prefect of the papal household, he or she is happy and full of hopeful joy. He or she is already certain of being able to see the Holy Father. How much more reason we have to be full of joy. We are baptized and we have received from the Heavenly Household, which has St. Peter as its prefect, a ticket to go to meet the Most Holy Trinity! This ticket is already in our pocket. At every moment, we are immersed in the immense and never-ending joy of hope.

Jesus said to the Hebrews: "Your ancestor Abraham rejoiced that he would see my day; he saw it and was glad" (Jn 8:56).

WORDS OF POPE JOHN PAUL II
At the Conclusion of the Spiritual Exercises

At the conclusion of these spiritual exercises, I thank the Lord who has given me the joy of sharing with you, dear and venerated brothers of the Roman Curia, these days of grace and of prayer. They have been days of intense and prolonged listening to the Spirit who has spoken to our hearts in silence and in attentive meditation of the Word of God. These have been days of a strong communitarian experience, which has given us a way to feel like the Apostles in the Cenacle, "constantly devoting themselves to prayer...together with Mary the mother of Jesus and with his brothers" (Acts 1:14).

In the name of everyone, I also thank the dearest Archbishop Francis Xavier Nguyễn Văn Thuận, President of the Pontifical Council for Justice and Peace. With simplicity and the breath of divine inspiration, he has guided us in deepening our vocation of witnessing to evangelical hope at the beginning of the Third Millennium. A witness of the cross in the long years of imprisonment in Vietnam, he has frequently recounted the realities and episodes from his sufferings in prison, thus reinforcing us in the consoling certainty that when everything crumbles around us, and perhaps even within us, Christ remains our unfailing support. We are grateful to Archbishop Văn Thuận—he who in prison was only Mr. Văn Thuận—for his witness, which is more meaningful than ever in this Jubilee Year.

Christ, Crucified and Risen, is our only true hope.

Strengthened by his help, even his disciples become men and women of hope—not a short-lived and fleeting hope that leaves the human heart tired and disappointed, but a true hope, a gift of God which, sustained from on high, strives to attain the highest good and is certain of reaching it. This hope is an urgent necessity for today's world.

The Great Jubilee that we are celebrating leads us step by step to deepening the reasons for this Christian hope that demands and fosters a growing trust in God and an always more generous openness to our brothers and sisters.

May Mary, Mother of hope, whom the homilist invited us to contemplate last night as the model of the Church, obtain for us the joy of hope. Thus, even in our moments of trial, as the travelers to Emmaus, the presence of Christ may change our sorrow into joy—"Your sorrow will be turned into joy."

With these sentiments, I bless you with my heart, asking all of you to continue to accompany me with prayer, above all for the pilgrimage to the Holy Land which, God willing, I will have the joy of making next week.

JOHN PAUL II

March 18, 2000

Other books by Francis Xavier Nguyễn Văn Thuận:

The Road of Hope (12 languages*)*

Pilgrims on the Road of Hope (4 languages)

The Road of Hope in the Light of God's Word and the Second Vatican Council (2 languages)

Prayers of Hope (3 languages)

Five Loaves and Two Fish (10 languages)

Testimony of Hope: Spiritual Exercises to John Paul II (8 languages in preparation)

Archbishop Văn Thuận has also published a number of additional titles in Vietnamese.

Pauline
BOOKS & MEDIA

The Daughters of St. Paul operate book and media centers at the following addresses. Visit, call or write the one nearest you today, or find us on the World Wide Web, www.pauline.org

CALIFORNIA
3908 Sepulveda Blvd., Culver City, CA 90230; 310-397-8676
5945 Balboa Ave., San Diego, CA 92111; 858-565-9181
46 Geary Street, San Francisco, CA 94108; 415-781-5180

FLORIDA
145 S.W. 107th Ave., Miami, FL 33174; 305-559-6715

HAWAII
1143 Bishop Street, Honolulu, HI 96813; 808-521-2731
Neighbor Islands call: 800-259-8463

ILLINOIS
172 North Michigan Ave., Chicago, IL 60601; 312-346-4228

LOUISIANA
4403 Veterans Memorial Blvd., Metairie, LA 70006; 504-887-7631

MASSACHUSETTS
Rte. 1, 885 Providence Hwy., Dedham, MA 02026; 781-326-5385

MISSOURI
9804 Watson Rd., St. Louis, MO 63126; 314-965-3512

NEW JERSEY
561 U.S. Route 1, Wick Plaza, Edison, NJ 08817; 732-572-1200

NEW YORK
150 East 52nd Street, New York, NY 10022; 212-754-1110
78 Fort Place, Staten Island, NY 10301; 718-447-5071

OHIO
2105 Ontario Street, Cleveland, OH 44115; 216-621-9427

PENNSYLVANIA
9171-A Roosevelt Blvd., Philadelphia, PA 19114; 215-676-9494

SOUTH CAROLINA
243 King Street, Charleston, SC 29401; 843-577-0175

TENNESSEE
4811 Poplar Ave., Memphis, TN 38117; 901-761-2987

TEXAS
114 Main Plaza, San Antonio, TX 78205; 210-224-8101

VIRGINIA
1025 King Street, Alexandria, VA 22314; 703-549-3806

CANADA
3022 Dufferin Street, Toronto, Ontario, Canada M6B 3T5; 416-781-9131
1155 Yonge Street, Toronto, Ontario, Canada M4T 1W2; 416-934-3440

¡También somos su fuente para libros, videos y música en español!